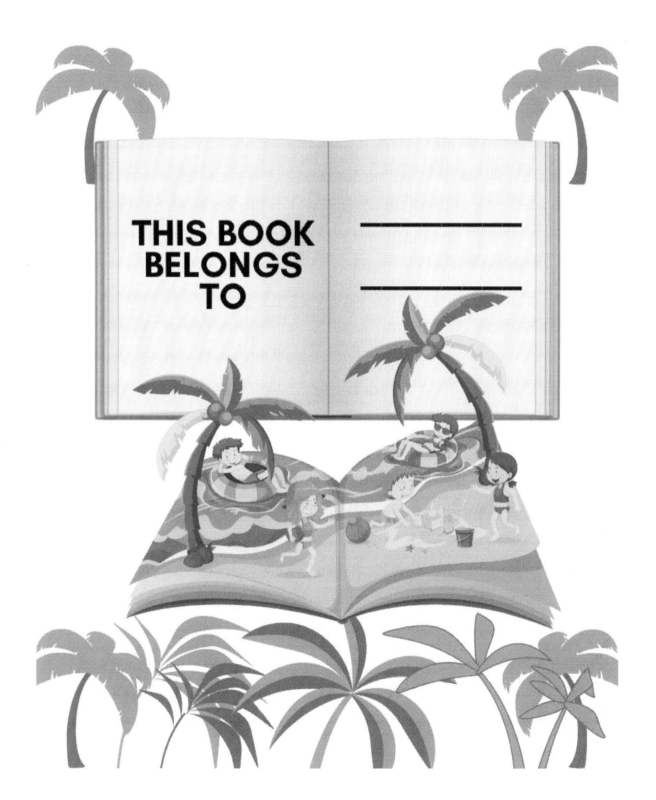

THIS BOOK BELONGS TO

____

____

The Summer Math Success: Math Workbook Grade 6-7 includes daily practice worksheets to enhance essential Math skills. This series is best for students to master important math concepts. After completing this workbook, the students will build problem solving and critical decision making skills and be able to recognize, understand the math problems and provide best possible solutions.

Moreover, this book is also best for teachers as well as parents to teach the basic and advanced math skills to children with daily math practice. This book is designed in a way that each worksheet can be graded with an opportunity to track the progress of the students.

Lastly, this book can be used in classroom for daily math activity, math practice, and math challenge or even for homework with parents. This book can also be used in **home-schooling by teachers and parents** for daily 20 to 30 minutes of Math Time.

We have provided the solutions for each worksheet in the back of the book to confirm the answers.

We hope you enjoy this summer with this wonderful book. Please also check our other Titles in the series.

Table of Contents

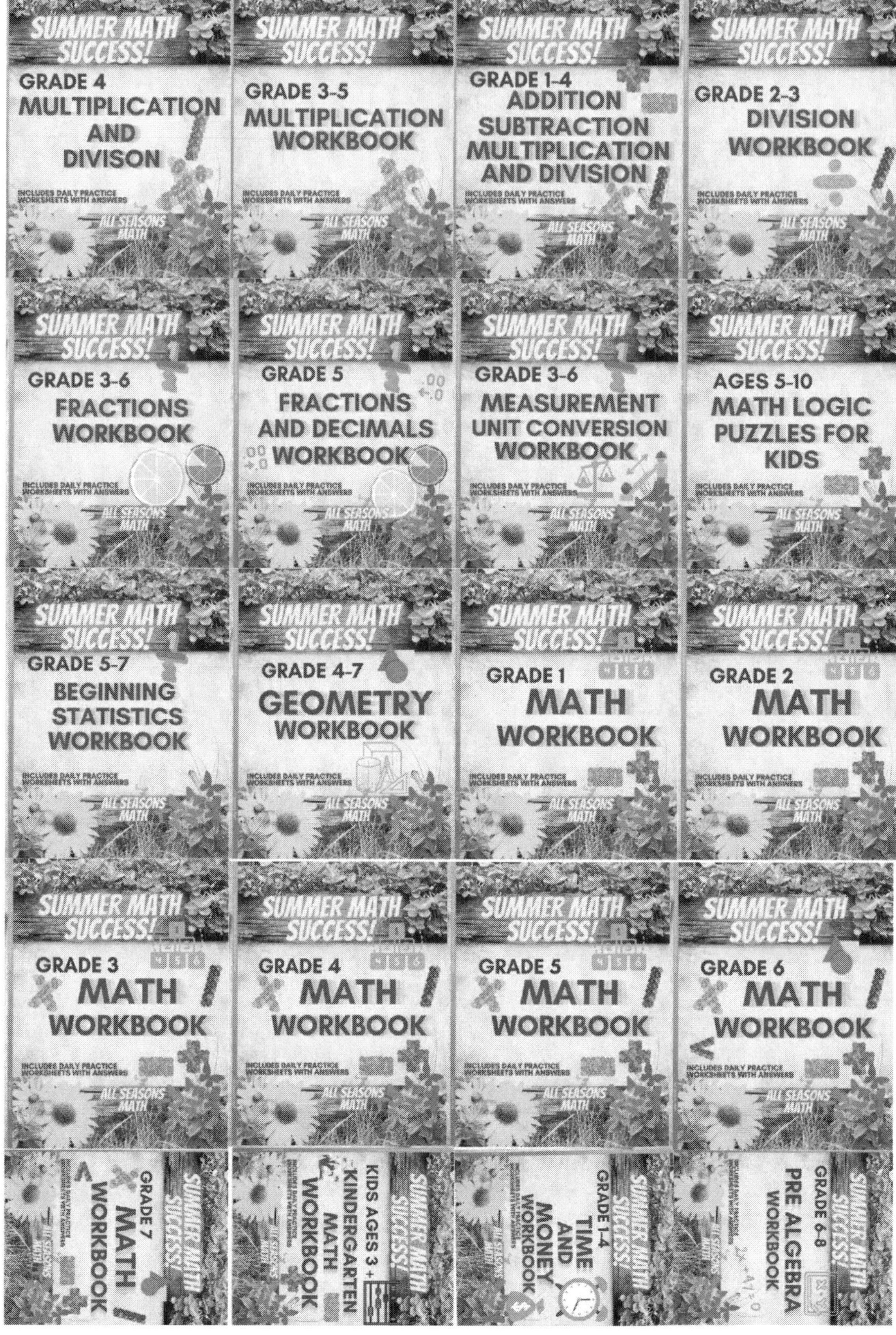
SUMMER MATH SUCCESS!
GRADE 4
MULTIPLICATION AND DIVISON
INCLUDES DAILY PRACTICE WORKSHEETS WITH ANSWERS
ALL SEASONS MATH
SUMMER MATH SUCCESS!
GRADE 3-5
MULTIPLICATION WORKBOOK
INCLUDES DAILY PRACTICE WORKSHEETS WITH ANSWERS
ALL SEASONS MATH
SUMMER MATH SUCCESS!
GRADE 1-4
ADDITION SUBTRACTION MULTIPLICATION AND DIVISION
INCLUDES DAILY PRACTICE WORKSHEETS WITH ANSWERS
ALL SEASONS MATH
SUMMER MATH SUCCESS!
GRADE 2-3
DIVISION WORKBOOK
INCLUDES DAILY PRACTICE WORKSHEETS WITH ANSWERS
ALL SEASONS MATH
SUMMER MATH SUCCESS!
GRADE 3-6
FRACTIONS WORKBOOK
INCLUDES DAILY PRACTICE WORKSHEETS WITH ANSWERS
ALL SEASONS MATH
SUMMER MATH SUCCESS!
GRADE 5
FRACTIONS AND DECIMALS WORKBOOK
INCLUDES DAILY PRACTICE WORKSHEETS WITH ANSWERS
ALL SEASONS MATH
SUMMER MATH SUCCESS!
GRADE 3-6
MEASUREMENT UNIT CONVERSION WORKBOOK
INCLUDES DAILY PRACTICE WORKSHEETS WITH ANSWERS
ALL SEASONS MATH
SUMMER MATH SUCCESS!
AGES 5-10
MATH LOGIC PUZZLES FOR KIDS
INCLUDES DAILY PRACTICE WORKSHEETS WITH ANSWERS
ALL SEASONS MATH
SUMMER MATH SUCCESS!
GRADE 5-7
BEGINNING STATISTICS WORKBOOK
INCLUDES DAILY PRACTICE WORKSHEETS WITH ANSWERS
ALL SEASONS MATH
SUMMER MATH SUCCESS!
GRADE 4-7
GEOMETRY WORKBOOK
INCLUDES DAILY PRACTICE WORKSHEETS WITH ANSWERS
ALL SEASONS MATH
SUMMER MATH SUCCESS!
GRADE 1
MATH WORKBOOK
INCLUDES DAILY PRACTICE WORKSHEETS WITH ANSWERS
ALL SEASONS MATH
SUMMER MATH SUCCESS!
GRADE 2
MATH WORKBOOK
INCLUDES DAILY PRACTICE WORKSHEETS WITH ANSWERS
ALL SEASONS MATH
SUMMER MATH SUCCESS!
GRADE 3
MATH WORKBOOK
INCLUDES DAILY PRACTICE WORKSHEETS WITH ANSWERS
ALL SEASONS MATH
SUMMER MATH SUCCESS!
GRADE 4
MATH WORKBOOK
INCLUDES DAILY PRACTICE WORKSHEETS WITH ANSWERS
ALL SEASONS MATH
SUMMER MATH SUCCESS!
GRADE 5
MATH WORKBOOK
INCLUDES DAILY PRACTICE WORKSHEETS WITH ANSWERS
ALL SEASONS MATH
SUMMER MATH SUCCESS!
GRADE 6
MATH WORKBOOK
INCLUDES DAILY PRACTICE WORKSHEETS WITH ANSWERS
ALL SEASONS MATH
SUMMER MATH SUCCESS!
GRADE 7
MATH WORKBOOK
SUMMER MATH SUCCESS!
KIDS AGES 3 +
KINDERGARTEN MATH WORKBOOK
SUMMER MATH SUCCESS!
GRADE 1-4
TIME AND MONEY WORKBOOK
SUMMER MATH SUCCESS!
GRADE 6-8
PRE ALGEBRA WORKBOOK

SUMMER
MATH SUCCESS

Name: ____________ Class: ________

Multiplication with Whole Numbers

Multiply.

1. $4 \times \frac{1}{3} =$ ____________
2. $\frac{2}{4}$ of $2 =$ ____________
3. $\frac{4}{5}$ of $9 =$ ____________
4. $8 \times \frac{3}{6} =$ ____________
5. $\frac{2}{8}$ of $6 =$ ____________
6. $5 \times \frac{1}{4} =$ ____________
7. $\frac{1}{5}$ of $8 =$ ____________
8. $2 \times \frac{4}{8} =$ ____________
9. $\frac{1}{3}$ of $6 =$ ____________
10. $4 \times \frac{1}{6} =$ ____________
11. $\frac{3}{4}$ of $7 =$ ____________
12. $4 \times \frac{2}{5} =$ ____________
13. $5 \times \frac{6}{8} =$ ____________
14. $\frac{4}{6}$ of $6 =$ ____________
15. $4 \times \frac{1}{3} =$ ____________
16. $\frac{1}{4}$ of $9 =$ ____________
17. $\frac{7}{8}$ of $6 =$ ____________
18. $7 \times \frac{3}{6} =$ ____________
19. $\frac{2}{5}$ of $2 =$ ____________
20. $7 \times \frac{2}{3} =$ ____________

SUMMER MATH SUCCESS

Name: ____________ Class: ________

Multiplication with Whole Numbers

Multiply.

(21) $7 \times \frac{1}{5} =$ ____________

(22) $\frac{1}{3}$ of $7 =$ ____________

(23) $\frac{7}{8}$ of $5 =$ ____________

(24) $\frac{1}{4}$ of $8 =$ ____________

(25) $\frac{2}{3}$ of $8 =$ ____________

(26) $1 \times \frac{4}{8} =$ ____________

(27) $\frac{1}{4}$ of $9 =$ ____________

(28) $\frac{1}{6}$ of $8 =$ ____________

(29) $\frac{4}{5}$ of $9 =$ ____________

(30) $5 \times \frac{2}{5} =$ ____________

(31) $\frac{3}{4}$ of $6 =$ ____________

(32) $5 \times \frac{1}{3} =$ ____________

(33) $8 \times \frac{4}{8} =$ ____________

(34) $3 \times \frac{2}{6} =$ ____________

(35) $\frac{3}{8}$ of $8 =$ ____________

(36) $6 \times \frac{2}{3} =$ ____________

(37) $7 \times \frac{2}{4} =$ ____________

(38) $\frac{2}{6}$ of $6 =$ ____________

(39) $1 \times \frac{2}{5} =$ ____________

(40) $4 \times \frac{2}{3} =$ ____________

SUMMER MATH SUCCESS

Name: ____________ Class: ________

Multiplication with Whole Numbers

Multiply.

(41) $5 \times \frac{2}{4} =$ ____________

(42) $4 \times \frac{2}{3} =$ ____________

(43) $\frac{3}{8}$ of $4 =$ ____________

(44) $\frac{4}{6}$ of $9 =$ ____________

(45) $\frac{2}{4}$ of $8 =$ ____________

(46) $7 \times \frac{7}{8} =$ ____________

(47) $3 \times \frac{3}{6} =$ ____________

(48) $\frac{2}{3}$ of $8 =$ ____________

(49) $5 \times \frac{1}{5} =$ ____________

(50) $2 \times \frac{1}{4} =$ ____________

(51) $\frac{1}{5}$ of $7 =$ ____________

(52) $\frac{4}{6}$ of $6 =$ ____________

(53) $5 \times \frac{4}{8} =$ ____________

(54) $4 \times \frac{1}{3} =$ ____________

(55) $\frac{2}{3}$ of $9 =$ ____________

(56) $6 \times \frac{5}{6} =$ ____________

(57) $4 \times \frac{1}{4} =$ ____________

(58) $\frac{7}{8}$ of $4 =$ ____________

(59) $7 \times \frac{1}{4} =$ ____________

(60) $3 \times \frac{2}{6} =$ ____________

SUMMER
MATH SUCCESS

Name: ____________ Class: ________

Division with Whole Numbers

Divide.

(61) $\frac{2}{3} \div 2 =$ ____________

(62) $\frac{2}{6} \div 6 =$ ____________

(63) $\frac{3}{4} \div 9 =$ ____________

(64) $\frac{7}{8} \div 3 =$ ____________

(65) $\frac{2}{6} \div 4 =$ ____________

(66) $\frac{1}{5} \div 4 =$ ____________

(67) $\frac{1}{3} \div 8 =$ ____________

(68) $\frac{3}{4} \div 1 =$ ____________

(69) $\frac{1}{6} \div 1 =$ ____________

(70) $\frac{1}{5} \div 8 =$ ____________

(71) $\frac{6}{8} \div 9 =$ ____________

(72) $\frac{1}{3} \div 2 =$ ____________

(73) $\frac{1}{4} \div 3 =$ ____________

(74) $\frac{4}{5} \div 2 =$ ____________

(75) $\frac{3}{8} \div 2 =$ ____________

(76) $\frac{2}{3} \div 8 =$ ____________

(77) $\frac{1}{6} \div 2 =$ ____________

(78) $\frac{6}{8} \div 1 =$ ____________

(79) $\frac{2}{5} \div 3 =$ ____________

(80) $\frac{2}{3} \div 1 =$ ____________

SUMMER MATH SUCCESS

Name: ______________ Class: __________

Division with Whole Numbers

Divide.

(81) $\frac{2}{5} \div 5 =$ ______________

(82) $\frac{1}{4} \div 1 =$ ______________

(83) $\frac{2}{5} \div 6 =$ ______________

(84) $\frac{4}{8} \div 4 =$ ______________

(85) $\frac{4}{6} \div 7 =$ ______________

(86) $\frac{2}{3} \div 2 =$ ______________

(87) $\frac{1}{4} \div 1 =$ ______________

(88) $\frac{3}{6} \div 3 =$ ______________

(89) $\frac{2}{4} \div 6 =$ ______________

(90) $\frac{6}{8} \div 9 =$ ______________

(91) $\frac{1}{3} \div 7 =$ ______________

(92) $\frac{1}{5} \div 7 =$ ______________

(93) $\frac{3}{5} \div 4 =$ ______________

(94) $\frac{4}{6} \div 9 =$ ______________

(95) $\frac{1}{3} \div 9 =$ ______________

(96) $\frac{2}{4} \div 6 =$ ______________

(97) $\frac{1}{8} \div 2 =$ ______________

(98) $\frac{4}{6} \div 7 =$ ______________

(99) $\frac{1}{3} \div 7 =$ ______________

(100) $\frac{4}{5} \div 4 =$ ______________

SUMMER
MATH SUCCESS

Name: ____________ Class: ________

Division with Whole Numbers

Divide.

(101) $\frac{3}{5} \div 8 =$ ________

(102) $\frac{3}{6} \div 1 =$ ________

(103) $\frac{1}{4} \div 2 =$ ________

(104) $\frac{1}{8} \div 6 =$ ________

(105) $\frac{3}{5} \div 9 =$ ________

(106) $\frac{2}{3} \div 2 =$ ________

(107) $\frac{2}{6} \div 5 =$ ________

(108) $\frac{1}{4} \div 1 =$ ________

(109) $\frac{2}{3} \div 6 =$ ________

(110) $\frac{5}{6} \div 6 =$ ________

(111) $\frac{3}{5} \div 4 =$ ________

(112) $\frac{4}{8} \div 6 =$ ________

(113) $\frac{2}{3} \div 1 =$ ________

(114) $\frac{3}{4} \div 5 =$ ________

(115) $\frac{3}{5} \div 4 =$ ________

(116) $\frac{3}{6} \div 7 =$ ________

(117) $\frac{1}{8} \div 2 =$ ________

(118) $\frac{1}{5} \div 9 =$ ________

(119) $\frac{1}{3} \div 4 =$ ________

(120) $\frac{2}{6} \div 8 =$ ________

SUMMER MATH SUCCESS

Name: ____________ Class: ________

Mixed Fractions - Multiplication

Calculate.

121. $1\frac{5}{7} \times 8\frac{1}{3} =$ ______________

122. $1\frac{3}{17} \times 9\frac{6}{8} =$ ______________

123. $1\frac{4}{19} \times 6\frac{3}{4} =$ ______________

124. $4\frac{6}{10} \times 5\frac{1}{2} =$ ______________

125. $1\frac{8}{23} \times 5\frac{22}{32} =$ ______________

126. $7\frac{2}{3} \times 7\frac{4}{12} =$ ______________

127. $9\frac{7}{15} \times 6\frac{27}{60} =$ ______________

128. $4\frac{10}{16} \times 1\frac{4}{13} =$ ______________

129. $2\frac{17}{21} \times 5\frac{3}{5} =$ ______________

130. $8\frac{14}{36} \times 2\frac{16}{100} =$ ______________

SUMMER
MATH SUCCESS

Name: ____________ Class: ________

Mixed Fractions - Multiplication

Calculate.

(131) $4\frac{10}{11} \times 6\frac{23}{32} =$ ____________

(132) $4\frac{4}{23} \times 9\frac{34}{50} =$ ____________

(133) $4\frac{1}{18} \times 8\frac{18}{20} =$ ____________

(134) $9\frac{5}{10} \times 2\frac{8}{21} =$ ____________

(135) $3\frac{16}{36} \times 4\frac{4}{8} =$ ____________

(136) $5\frac{34}{75} \times 7\frac{13}{14} =$ ____________

(137) $1\frac{4}{6} \times 8\frac{12}{13} =$ ____________

(138) $7\frac{1}{2} \times 1\frac{2}{3} =$ ____________

(139) $2\frac{34}{100} \times 2\frac{3}{20} =$ ____________

(140) $8\frac{14}{15} \times 9\frac{3}{75} =$ ____________

SUMMER MATH SUCCESS

Name: ________________ Class: __________

Mixed Fractions - Multiplication

Calculate.

(141) $5\frac{1}{22} \times 7\frac{29}{50} =$ ______________________

(142) $9\frac{23}{60} \times 7\frac{2}{3} =$ ______________________

(143) $9\frac{2}{7} \times 4\frac{9}{20} =$ ______________________

(144) $8\frac{21}{32} \times 9\frac{2}{4} =$ ______________________

(145) $2\frac{3}{5} \times 9\frac{7}{15} =$ ______________________

(146) $3\frac{12}{13} \times 2\frac{11}{30} =$ ______________________

(147) $5\frac{4}{6} \times 2\frac{15}{21} =$ ______________________

(148) $8\frac{11}{19} \times 3\frac{3}{10} =$ ______________________

(149) $4\frac{1}{16} \times 4\frac{17}{24} =$ ______________________

(150) $7\frac{1}{12} \times 8\frac{5}{17} =$ ______________________

SUMMER MATH SUCCESS

Name: ____________ Class: ________

Mixed Fractions- Division

Calculate.

(151) $5\frac{9}{10} \div 6\frac{6}{19} =$ ______________

(152) $7\frac{1}{16} \div 8\frac{4}{18} =$ ______________

(153) $5\frac{7}{8} \div 7\frac{63}{75} =$ ______________

(154) $2\frac{4}{5} \div 5\frac{4}{13} =$ ______________

(155) $8\frac{2}{36} \div 6\frac{27}{36} =$ ______________

(156) $9\frac{11}{60} \div 6\frac{2}{3} =$ ______________

(157) $8\frac{1}{7} \div 9\frac{39}{100} =$ ______________

(158) $9\frac{29}{30} \div 9\frac{6}{18} =$ ______________

(159) $9\frac{1}{12} \div 5\frac{31}{50} =$ ______________

(160) $3\frac{15}{25} \div 7\frac{14}{19} =$ ______________

SUMMER MATH SUCCESS

Name: ____________ Class: ________

Mixed Fractions- Division

Calculate.

(161) $2\frac{3}{11} \div 5\frac{3}{21} =$ ____________

(162) $4\frac{1}{2} \div 7\frac{6}{7} =$ ____________

(163) $6\frac{33}{36} \div 7\frac{1}{6} =$ ____________

(164) $8\frac{3}{10} \div 3\frac{11}{13} =$ ____________

(165) $5\frac{13}{30} \div 3\frac{2}{3} =$ ____________

(166) $8\frac{12}{40} \div 6\frac{9}{15} =$ ____________

(167) $7\frac{4}{5} \div 6\frac{18}{25} =$ ____________

(168) $5\frac{1}{12} \div 2\frac{3}{23} =$ ____________

(169) $1\frac{13}{24} \div 3\frac{26}{60} =$ ____________

(170) $4\frac{5}{17} \div 1\frac{8}{75} =$ ____________

SUMMER MATH SUCCESS

Name: ____________ Class: ________

Mixed Fractions- Division

Calculate.

(171) $8\frac{12}{16} \div 1\frac{4}{22} =$ ____________

(172) $1\frac{8}{15} \div 9\frac{63}{100} =$ ____________

(173) $2\frac{2}{8} \div 2\frac{20}{22} =$ ____________

(174) $3\frac{34}{36} \div 8\frac{5}{9} =$ ____________

(175) $3\frac{4}{10} \div 6\frac{2}{3} =$ ____________

(176) $8\frac{10}{21} \div 4\frac{38}{75} =$ ____________

(177) $7\frac{10}{11} \div 8\frac{7}{14} =$ ____________

(178) $7\frac{9}{20} \div 8\frac{8}{19} =$ ____________

(179) $1\frac{23}{25} \div 4\frac{11}{16} =$ ____________

(180) $8\frac{3}{6} \div 1\frac{5}{7} =$ ____________

SUMMER MATH SUCCESS

Name: ________________ Class: __________

Fractions: Multiple Operations

Find the solution.

(181) $(\frac{1}{6} + \frac{5}{6}) \div \frac{1}{6} =$ ________________

(182) $(\frac{2}{3} \times \frac{2}{3}) + (\frac{2}{3} \times \frac{2}{3}) =$ ________________

(183) $\frac{5}{8} + \frac{7}{8} + \frac{7}{8} + \frac{1}{8} =$ ________________

(184) $(\frac{2}{5} + \frac{4}{5}) \div \frac{3}{5} =$ ________________

(185) $\frac{1}{8} \times \frac{5}{8} \times \frac{3}{8} =$ ________________

(186) $(\frac{4}{5} + \frac{2}{5}) \div \frac{4}{5} =$ ________________

(187) $\frac{3}{5} + \frac{1}{4} + \frac{1}{5} + \frac{3}{4} =$ ________________

(188) $\frac{5}{8} + \frac{3}{8} + \frac{1}{8} =$ ________________

(189) $\frac{1}{4} + \frac{1}{5} + 2 =$ ________________

(190) $\frac{1}{4} + \frac{1}{4} + \frac{1}{4} =$ ________________

SUMMER MATH SUCCESS

Name: ____________ Class: ________

Fractions: Multiple Operations

Find the solution.

(191) $(\frac{5}{6} \times \frac{3}{8}) + (\frac{1}{6} \times \frac{1}{8}) =$ ____________

(192) $\frac{3}{8} + \frac{3}{8} + \frac{1}{8} =$ ____________

(193) $(\frac{3}{4} + \frac{3}{4}) - (\frac{1}{4} \times \frac{1}{4}) =$ ____________

(194) $\frac{4}{5} + \frac{2}{5} + \frac{1}{5} =$ ____________

(195) $\frac{3}{8} + \frac{2}{5} - \frac{3}{8} =$ ____________

(196) $(\frac{1}{4} \times \frac{1}{3}) + (\frac{1}{4} \times \frac{2}{3}) =$ ____________

(197) $(\frac{3}{8} + \frac{7}{8}) - (\frac{4}{5} \times \frac{2}{5}) =$ ____________

(198) $\frac{1}{3} + \frac{1}{3} + \frac{1}{3} =$ ____________

(199) $(\frac{1}{6} + \frac{1}{6}) \times (\frac{5}{6} + \frac{5}{6}) =$ ____________

(200) $(\frac{3}{5} + \frac{2}{5}) \div \frac{4}{5} =$ ____________

SUMMER MATH SUCCESS

Name: ____________ Class: ________

Fractions: Multiple Operations

Find the solution.

201 $\frac{1}{4} + \frac{1}{5} + \frac{1}{4} + \frac{1}{5} =$ ____________

202 $\frac{3}{8} + \frac{1}{8} + \frac{7}{8} =$ ____________

203 $\frac{4}{5} \times \frac{2}{5} \times \frac{3}{5} =$ ____________

204 $\frac{1}{3} + \frac{1}{4} + \frac{1}{3} + \frac{1}{4} =$ ____________

205 $(\frac{1}{4} \times \frac{7}{8}) + (\frac{3}{4} \times \frac{5}{8}) =$ ____________

206 $\frac{1}{5} + \frac{2}{5} + \frac{3}{5} =$ ____________

207 $\frac{3}{5} \times \frac{1}{4} + \frac{3}{4} =$ ____________

208 $\frac{1}{6} \times \frac{1}{6} + \frac{5}{6} =$ ____________

209 $\frac{2}{5} \times \frac{1}{5} + \frac{1}{5} =$ ____________

210 $\frac{3}{8} + \frac{1}{8} + \frac{1}{8} =$ ____________

SUMMER
MATH SUCCESS

Name: ____________ Class: ________

Fractions: Multiple Operations

Find the solution.

(211) $\frac{1}{6} \times \frac{1}{6} \times \frac{1}{6} =$ ____________

(212) $\frac{1}{6} \times \frac{1}{6} + \frac{5}{6} =$ ____________

(213) $\frac{1}{4} + \frac{5}{8} + 4 =$ ____________

(214) $(\frac{5}{8} + \frac{1}{8}) \times (\frac{3}{8} + \frac{7}{8}) =$ ____________

(215) $\frac{1}{4} \times \frac{3}{4} \times \frac{1}{4} =$ ____________

(216) $(\frac{1}{6} + \frac{5}{6}) \div \frac{1}{6} =$ ____________

(217) $\frac{2}{3} + \frac{4}{5} + 4 =$ ____________

(218) $\frac{3}{8} \times \frac{1}{8} + \frac{7}{8} =$ ____________

(219) $\frac{4}{5} + \frac{1}{6} + \frac{1}{5} + \frac{1}{6} =$ ____________

(220) $(\frac{3}{5} + \frac{1}{5}) - (\frac{1}{4} \times \frac{3}{4}) =$ ____________

SUMMER
MATH SUCCESS

Name: ______________ Class: __________

Fractions: Multiple Operations
Find the solution.

(221) $\frac{1}{5} \times \frac{1}{5} + \frac{1}{5} =$ ____________________

(222) $(\frac{5}{6} + \frac{1}{6}) \times (\frac{1}{6} + \frac{5}{6}) =$ ____________________

(223) $\frac{3}{4} \times \frac{3}{4} + \frac{1}{4} =$ ____________________

(224) $(\frac{1}{5} + \frac{4}{5}) \times (\frac{2}{5} + \frac{1}{5}) =$ ____________________

(225) $\frac{1}{6} \times \frac{1}{6} \times \frac{1}{6} =$ ____________________

(226) $(\frac{2}{3} + \frac{1}{3}) \times (\frac{1}{3} + \frac{1}{3}) =$ ____________________

(227) $\frac{1}{6} + \frac{4}{5} + \frac{5}{6} + \frac{2}{5} =$ ____________________

(228) $\frac{4}{5} + \frac{1}{3} + \frac{3}{5} + \frac{2}{3} =$ ____________________

(229) $\frac{1}{6} + \frac{1}{6} + \frac{1}{6} =$ ____________________

(230) $\frac{2}{3} + \frac{1}{3} + \frac{2}{3} =$ ____________________

SUMMER MATH SUCCESS

Name: ____________ Class: ________

Fractions: Multiple Operations

Find the solution.

231 $\frac{1}{3} + \frac{3}{8} - \frac{2}{3} =$ ____________

232 $\frac{1}{3} \times \frac{1}{3} + \frac{1}{3} =$ ____________

233 $\frac{3}{4} \times \frac{1}{4} + \frac{1}{4} =$ ____________

234 $\frac{3}{8} + \frac{1}{6} + 5 =$ ____________

235 $(\frac{2}{3} \times \frac{1}{6}) + (\frac{1}{3} \times \frac{1}{6}) =$ ____________

236 $\frac{1}{5} + \frac{4}{5} + 3 =$ ____________

237 $\frac{2}{3} \times \frac{1}{6} + \frac{1}{6} =$ ____________

238 $\frac{1}{6} + \frac{5}{8} + \frac{1}{6} + \frac{3}{8} =$ ____________

239 $\frac{1}{4} \times \frac{2}{3} + \frac{2}{3} =$ ____________

240 $(\frac{1}{6} + \frac{1}{6}) \times (\frac{1}{6} + \frac{5}{6}) =$ ____________

SUMMER MATH SUCCESS

Name: ____________ Class: ________

Fractions: Multiple Operations

Find the solution.

(241) $(\frac{1}{3} + \frac{1}{3}) \times (\frac{1}{3} + \frac{2}{3}) =$ ____________

(242) $\frac{1}{4} + \frac{1}{4} + \frac{3}{4} =$ ____________

(243) $(\frac{2}{3} + \frac{1}{3}) - (\frac{3}{5} \times \frac{2}{5}) =$ ____________

(244) $(\frac{1}{8} + \frac{1}{8}) - (\frac{1}{4} \times \frac{1}{4}) =$ ____________

(245) $\frac{1}{6} + \frac{2}{3} + 6 =$ ____________

(246) $\frac{1}{6} + \frac{3}{8} - \frac{1}{6} =$ ____________

(247) $\frac{1}{4} \times \frac{3}{4} \times \frac{1}{4} =$ ____________

(248) $\frac{7}{8} \times \frac{7}{8} \times \frac{5}{8} =$ ____________

(249) $\frac{1}{3} + \frac{5}{6} + 4 =$ ____________

(250) $\frac{5}{8} + \frac{3}{4} + 9 =$ ____________

SUMMER MATH SUCCESS

Name: ________________ Class: __________

Fractions: Multiple Operations

Find the solution.

251) $(\frac{5}{8} + \frac{3}{8}) - (\frac{1}{6} \times \frac{1}{6}) =$ ____________________

252) $(\frac{3}{5} + \frac{3}{5}) \div \frac{4}{5} =$ ____________________

253) $(\frac{1}{4} + \frac{1}{4}) \times (\frac{1}{4} + \frac{3}{4}) =$ ____________________

254) $(\frac{1}{3} + \frac{1}{3}) - (\frac{1}{4} \times \frac{3}{4}) =$ ____________________

255) $\frac{3}{5} + \frac{1}{5} + 7 =$ ____________________

256) $\frac{5}{8} + \frac{1}{3} - \frac{5}{8} =$ ____________________

257) $\frac{1}{8} \times \frac{1}{8} + \frac{3}{8} =$ ____________________

258) $(\frac{1}{6} + \frac{1}{6}) \times (\frac{1}{6} + \frac{1}{6}) =$ ____________________

259) $(\frac{1}{6} + \frac{1}{6}) - (\frac{5}{6} \times \frac{1}{6}) =$ ____________________

260) $(\frac{1}{3} + \frac{1}{3}) \div \frac{2}{3} =$ ____________________

SUMMER
MATH SUCCESS

Name: ____________ Class: ________

Fractions: Multiple Operations

Find the solution.

(261) $(\frac{1}{8} + \frac{3}{8}) \times (\frac{7}{8} + \frac{1}{8}) =$ ____________

(262) $(\frac{7}{8} + \frac{5}{8}) - (\frac{3}{4} \times \frac{3}{4}) =$ ____________

(263) $\frac{5}{8} \times \frac{4}{5} + \frac{1}{5} =$ ____________

(264) $(\frac{3}{8} + \frac{5}{8}) - (\frac{1}{4} \times \frac{3}{4}) =$ ____________

(265) $(\frac{1}{6} \times \frac{1}{6}) + (\frac{5}{6} \times \frac{5}{6}) =$ ____________

(266) $\frac{1}{8} + \frac{3}{8} + \frac{3}{8} + \frac{5}{8} =$ ____________

(267) $(\frac{1}{4} + \frac{1}{4}) \div \frac{1}{4} =$ ____________

(268) $(\frac{1}{3} + \frac{1}{3}) \div \frac{1}{3} =$ ____________

(269) $\frac{2}{5} + \frac{4}{5} + \frac{3}{5} + \frac{1}{5} =$ ____________

(270) $\frac{1}{6} + \frac{1}{6} - \frac{1}{6} =$ ____________

SUMMER
MATH SUCCESS

Name: ____________ Class: ________

Fractions: Multiple Operations

Find the solution.

271 $\frac{1}{8} + \frac{3}{8} + 9 =$ ____________

272 $\frac{1}{6} + \frac{2}{3} + \frac{1}{6} + \frac{1}{3} =$ ____________

273 $\frac{3}{8} + \frac{1}{8} + \frac{1}{8} =$ ____________

274 $\frac{2}{3} + \frac{2}{5} + 7 =$ ____________

275 $\frac{1}{3} \times \frac{1}{6} + \frac{5}{6} =$ ____________

276 $\frac{1}{4} \times \frac{1}{8} + \frac{1}{8} =$ ____________

277 $(\frac{5}{6} + \frac{1}{6}) - (\frac{2}{3} \times \frac{1}{3}) =$ ____________

278 $\frac{1}{4} + \frac{1}{4} + \frac{1}{4} =$ ____________

279 $(\frac{1}{3} + \frac{1}{3}) - (\frac{2}{3} \times \frac{2}{3}) =$ ____________

280 $(\frac{1}{6} + \frac{1}{6}) - (\frac{1}{6} \times \frac{1}{6}) =$ ____________

SUMMER
MATH SUCCESS

Name: ____________ Class: ________

Simplifying Fractions

(281) $\frac{954}{135} =$ ____________

(282) $\frac{558}{90} =$ ____________

(283) $\frac{96}{112} =$ ____________

(284) $\frac{4}{12} =$ ____________

(285) $\frac{84}{12} =$ ____________

(286) $\frac{136}{16} =$ ____________

(287) $\frac{648}{72} =$ ____________

(288) $\frac{6}{18} =$ ____________

(289) $\frac{441}{90} =$ ____________

(290) $\frac{216}{24} =$ ____________

(291) $\frac{10}{25} =$ ____________

(292) $\frac{27}{54} =$ ____________

(293) $\frac{320}{112} =$ ____________

(294) $\frac{210}{30} =$ ____________

(295) $\frac{120}{20} =$ ____________

(296) $\frac{749}{105} =$ ____________

(297) $\frac{360}{40} =$ ____________

(298) $\frac{40}{48} =$ ____________

(299) $\frac{678}{84} =$ ____________

(300) $\frac{4}{10} =$ ____________

SUMMER MATH SUCCESS

Name: ____________ Class: ________

Simplifying Fractions

(301) $\frac{10}{5}$ = ____________

(302) $\frac{155}{30}$ = ____________

(303) $\frac{120}{18}$ = ____________

(304) $\frac{420}{84}$ = ____________

(305) $\frac{392}{56}$ = ____________

(306) $\frac{66}{18}$ = ____________

(307) $\frac{240}{60}$ = ____________

(308) $\frac{360}{120}$ = ____________

(309) $\frac{594}{72}$ = ____________

(310) $\frac{4}{24}$ = ____________

(311) $\frac{333}{45}$ = ____________

(312) $\frac{208}{24}$ = ____________

(313) $\frac{24}{32}$ = ____________

(314) $\frac{3}{36}$ = ____________

(315) $\frac{60}{30}$ = ____________

(316) $\frac{270}{75}$ = ____________

(317) $\frac{120}{20}$ = ____________

(318) $\frac{144}{18}$ = ____________

(319) $\frac{448}{56}$ = ____________

(320) $\frac{54}{72}$ = ____________

SUMMER
MATH SUCCESS

Name: ______________ Class: __________

Simplifying Fractions

(321) $\frac{891}{108}$ = ____________

(322) $\frac{245}{35}$ = ____________

(323) $\frac{3}{9}$ = ____________

(324) $\frac{16}{40}$ = ____________

(325) $\frac{504}{84}$ = ____________

(326) $\frac{240}{64}$ = ____________

(327) $\frac{9}{12}$ = ____________

(328) $\frac{36}{40}$ = ____________

(329) $\frac{195}{75}$ = ____________

(330) $\frac{192}{48}$ = ____________

(331) $\frac{99}{108}$ = ____________

(332) $\frac{90}{18}$ = ____________

(333) $\frac{108}{12}$ = ____________

(334) $\frac{81}{108}$ = ____________

(335) $\frac{588}{98}$ = ____________

(336) $\frac{18}{24}$ = ____________

(337) $\frac{70}{16}$ = ____________

(338) $\frac{24}{60}$ = ____________

(339) $\frac{174}{30}$ = ____________

(340) $\frac{120}{60}$ = ____________

SUMMER MATH SUCCESS

Name: ____________ Class: ________

Simplifying Fractions

(341) $\frac{48}{56} =$ ____________

(342) $\frac{1120}{120} =$ ____________

(343) $\frac{196}{42} =$ ____________

(344) $\frac{126}{18} =$ ____________

(345) $\frac{35}{50} =$ ____________

(346) $\frac{145}{20} =$ ____________

(347) $\frac{88}{96} =$ ____________

(348) $\frac{156}{20} =$ ____________

(349) $\frac{192}{64} =$ ____________

(350) $\frac{672}{105} =$ ____________

(351) $\frac{12}{32} =$ ____________

(352) $\frac{192}{24} =$ ____________

(353) $\frac{648}{72} =$ ____________

(354) $\frac{145}{70} =$ ____________

(355) $\frac{18}{9} =$ ____________

(356) $\frac{192}{20} =$ ____________

(357) $\frac{66}{20} =$ ____________

(358) $\frac{720}{90} =$ ____________

(359) $\frac{135}{15} =$ ____________

(360) $\frac{75}{15} =$ ____________

SUMMER MATH SUCCESS

Name: ____________ Class: ________

Simplifying Fractions

(361) $\frac{2}{6} =$ ____________

(362) $\frac{94}{28} =$ ____________

(363) $\frac{45}{54} =$ ____________

(364) $\frac{6}{12} =$ ____________

(365) $\frac{312}{96} =$ ____________

(366) $\frac{8}{80} =$ ____________

(367) $\frac{15}{30} =$ ____________

(368) $\frac{384}{48} =$ ____________

(369) $\frac{46}{6} =$ ____________

(370) $\frac{112}{48} =$ ____________

(371) $\frac{298}{30} =$ ____________

(372) $\frac{8}{32} =$ ____________

(373) $\frac{140}{28} =$ ____________

(374) $\frac{32}{64} =$ ____________

(375) $\frac{14}{35} =$ ____________

(376) $\frac{252}{126} =$ ____________

(377) $\frac{64}{96} =$ ____________

(378) $\frac{24}{6} =$ ____________

(379) $\frac{5}{30} =$ ____________

(380) $\frac{24}{32} =$ ____________

SUMMER
MATH SUCCESS

Name: ____________________ Class: __________

Simplifying Fractions

(381) $\frac{54}{14}$ = ____________________

(382) $\frac{42}{56}$ = ____________________

(383) $\frac{6}{24}$ = ____________________

(384) $\frac{198}{20}$ = ____________________

(385) $\frac{36}{126}$ = ____________________

(386) $\frac{244}{60}$ = ____________________

(387) $\frac{413}{56}$ = ____________________

(388) $\frac{315}{90}$ = ____________________

(389) $\frac{9}{18}$ = ____________________

(390) $\frac{352}{40}$ = ____________________

(391) $\frac{432}{108}$ = ____________________

(392) $\frac{153}{27}$ = ____________________

(393) $\frac{7}{28}$ = ____________________

(394) $\frac{192}{48}$ = ____________________

(395) $\frac{152}{20}$ = ____________________

(396) $\frac{7}{56}$ = ____________________

(397) $\frac{525}{75}$ = ____________________

(398) $\frac{30}{15}$ = ____________________

(399) $\frac{48}{12}$ = ____________________

(400) $\frac{164}{56}$ = ____________________

SUMMER MATH SUCCESS

Name: ______________ Class: __________

Simplifying Fractions

401. $\frac{18}{27} =$ ______________

402. $\frac{105}{42} =$ ______________

403. $\frac{24}{32} =$ ______________

404. $\frac{160}{60} =$ ______________

405. $\frac{468}{84} =$ ______________

406. $\frac{90}{15} =$ ______________

407. $\frac{704}{80} =$ ______________

408. $\frac{329}{105} =$ ______________

409. $\frac{42}{48} =$ ______________

410. $\frac{144}{24} =$ ______________

411. $\frac{420}{70} =$ ______________

412. $\frac{472}{80} =$ ______________

413. $\frac{108}{27} =$ ______________

414. $\frac{196}{28} =$ ______________

415. $\frac{520}{120} =$ ______________

416. $\frac{480}{60} =$ ______________

417. $\frac{126}{24} =$ ______________

418. $\frac{72}{15} =$ ______________

419. $\frac{36}{8} =$ ______________

420. $\frac{210}{105} =$ ______________

SUMMER
MATH SUCCESS

Name: ____________ Class: ________

Simplifying Fractions

421) $\frac{168}{24} =$ ____________

422) $\frac{235}{70} =$ ____________

423) $\frac{96}{12} =$ ____________

424) $\frac{405}{45} =$ ____________

425) $\frac{64}{80} =$ ____________

426) $\frac{90}{15} =$ ____________

427) $\frac{144}{16} =$ ____________

428) $\frac{21}{42} =$ ____________

429) $\frac{96}{42} =$ ____________

430) $\frac{72}{20} =$ ____________

431) $\frac{238}{70} =$ ____________

432) $\frac{56}{12} =$ ____________

433) $\frac{48}{24} =$ ____________

434) $\frac{155}{40} =$ ____________

435) $\frac{140}{60} =$ ____________

436) $\frac{648}{108} =$ ____________

437) $\frac{4}{40} =$ ____________

438) $\frac{5}{25} =$ ____________

439) $\frac{4}{8} =$ ____________

440) $\frac{511}{84} =$ ____________

SUMMER MATH SUCCESS

Name: ____________ Class: ________

Simplifying Fractions

(441) $\frac{200}{40}$ = ____________

(442) $\frac{16}{48}$ = ____________

(443) $\frac{196}{28}$ = ____________

(444) $\frac{540}{108}$ = ____________

(445) $\frac{80}{40}$ = ____________

(446) $\frac{52}{8}$ = ____________

(447) $\frac{162}{24}$ = ____________

(448) $\frac{322}{98}$ = ____________

(449) $\frac{540}{90}$ = ____________

(450) $\frac{98}{10}$ = ____________

(451) $\frac{162}{20}$ = ____________

(452) $\frac{320}{48}$ = ____________

(453) $\frac{12}{18}$ = ____________

(454) $\frac{56}{84}$ = ____________

(455) $\frac{217}{35}$ = ____________

(456) $\frac{36}{42}$ = ____________

(457) $\frac{63}{108}$ = ____________

(458) $\frac{12}{24}$ = ____________

(459) $\frac{8}{12}$ = ____________

(460) $\frac{324}{40}$ = ____________

SUMMER MATH SUCCESS

Name: ____________ Class: ________

Simplifying Fractions

(461) $\frac{75}{12}$ = ______________

(462) $\frac{92}{12}$ = ______________

(463) $\frac{62}{10}$ = ______________

(464) $\frac{20}{30}$ = ______________

(465) $\frac{60}{72}$ = ______________

(466) $\frac{350}{70}$ = ______________

(467) $\frac{24}{30}$ = ______________

(468) $\frac{66}{24}$ = ______________

(469) $\frac{868}{98}$ = ______________

(470) $\frac{154}{21}$ = ______________

(471) $\frac{120}{24}$ = ______________

(472) $\frac{432}{54}$ = ______________

(473) $\frac{455}{75}$ = ______________

(474) $\frac{48}{16}$ = ______________

(475) $\frac{150}{50}$ = ______________

(476) $\frac{18}{108}$ = ______________

(477) $\frac{32}{12}$ = ______________

(478) $\frac{324}{36}$ = ______________

(479) $\frac{28}{35}$ = ______________

(480) $\frac{230}{28}$ = ______________

SUMMER MATH SUCCESS

Name: ____________ Class: ________

Percent

Find the percentage of given numbers and percent values.

(481) ☐ of 75 = 7.5

(482) 8% of ☐ = 27.76

(483) 20% of 328 = ☐

(484) 10% of ☐ = 51.4

(485) 5% of ☐ = 13.15

(486) 25% of 1 = ☐

(487) ☐ of 270 = 40.5

(488) 2% of ☐ = 1.46

(489) ☐ of 899 = 71.92

(490) 15% of 647 = ☐

(491) ☐ of 881 = 176.2

(492) ☐ of 808 = 202

(493) 15% of ☐ = 80.25

(494) 8% of ☐ = 74.16

(495) ☐ of 579 = 57.9

(496) 20% of ☐ = 77

(497) 5% of 165 = ☐

(498) 2% of ☐ = 14.52

(499) 5% of 268 = ☐

(500) 8% of 411 = ☐

SUMMER MATH SUCCESS

Name: ____________ Class: ________

Percent

Find the percentage of given numbers and percent values.

501. 20% of 12 = ____
502. 25% of 86 = ____
503. 10% of 950 = ____
504. ____ of 9 = 1.35
505. 8% of 950 = ____
506. 10% of ____ = 2.6
507. 5% of 944 = ____
508. ____ of 259 = 51.8
509. 15% of ____ = 51.9
510. 25% of 971 = ____
511. ____ of 873 = 69.84
512. 2% of 527 = ____
513. 15% of 687 = ____
514. ____ of 674 = 134.8
515. ____ of 14 = 0.7
516. 10% of 636 = ____
517. 25% of ____ = 96.5
518. 2% of ____ = 16.42
519. 8% of ____ = 64
520. ____ of 133 = 6.65

SUMMER MATH SUCCESS

Name: ______________ Class: __________

Percent

Find the percentage of given numbers and percent values.

(521) ☐ of 241 = 48.2

(522) 15% of 103 = ☐

(523) ☐ of 467 = 23.35

(524) 2% of 505 = ☐

(525) 8% of ☐ = 14

(526) ☐ of 259 = 64.75

(527) 5% of ☐ = 30.65

(528) 10% of ☐ = 10.8

(529) 2% of 129 = ☐

(530) 15% of ☐ = 79.5

(531) ☐ of 618 = 154.5

(532) ☐ of 271 = 21.68

(533) 20% of ☐ = 163.8

(534) 10% of ☐ = 73.6

(535) 15% of 87 = ☐

(536) 2% of ☐ = 9.92

(537) 20% of 554 = ☐

(538) 25% of ☐ = 88.25

(539) 8% of 769 = ☐

(540) ☐ of 311 = 15.55

SUMMER
MATH SUCCESS

Name: ____________ Class: ________

Percent

Find the percentage of given numbers and percent values.

541 ☐ of 282 = 14.1

542 ☐ of 219 = 4.38

543 10% of 919 = ☐

544 8% of ☐ = 6.88

545 15% of 676 = ☐

546 20% of ☐ = 195.2

547 25% of ☐ = 164

548 ☐ of 536 = 10.72

549 ☐ of 441 = 88.2

550 ☐ of 742 = 37.1

551 ☐ of 770 = 115.5

552 ☐ of 861 = 68.88

553 10% of 813 = ☐

554 25% of ☐ = 171.25

555 8% of ☐ = 33.12

556 ☐ of 263 = 39.45

557 2% of 328 = ☐

558 10% of 680 = ☐

559 25% of ☐ = 84.25

560 5% of ☐ = 43.65

SUMMER MATH SUCCESS

Name: ________________ Class: __________

Percent

Find the percentage of given numbers and percent values.

(561) 15% of 692 = ☐

(562) 8% of ☐ = 10.08

(563) ☐ of 804 = 160.8

(564) ☐ of 886 = 44.3

(565) 10% of ☐ = 18.3

(566) 25% of 270 = ☐

(567) ☐ of 533 = 79.95

(568) 2% of ☐ = 13.66

(569) ☐ of 545 = 109

(570) 2% of 642 = ☐

(571) ☐ of 882 = 220.5

(572) 15% of 176 = ☐

(573) 8% of ☐ = 74.88

(574) 5% of ☐ = 31.55

(575) ☐ of 134 = 13.4

(576) ☐ of 322 = 16.1

(577) 2% of 527 = ☐

(578) 8% of ☐ = 52.64

(579) 25% of 69 = ☐

(580) ☐ of 312 = 31.2

SUMMER
MATH SUCCESS

Name: ____________ Class: ________

Percent and Decimals

Convert Percent to Decimal.

(581) 86 % = ____________

(582) 38 % = ____________

(583) 13 % = ____________

(584) 62 % = ____________

(585) 48 % = ____________

(586) 78 % = ____________

(587) 47 % = ____________

(588) 79 % = ____________

(589) 93 % = ____________

(590) 63 % = ____________

(591) 14 % = ____________

(592) 98 % = ____________

(593) 31 % = ____________

(594) 10 % = ____________

(595) 80 % = ____________

(596) 83 % = ____________

(597) 24 % = ____________

(598) 11 % = ____________

(599) 40 % = ____________

(600) 16 % = ____________

SUMMER
MATH SUCCESS

Name: ______________ Class: __________

Percent and Decimals

Convert Percent to Decimal.

(601) 22 % = ______________

(602) 78 % = ______________

(603) 34 % = ______________

(604) 61 % = ______________

(605) 56 % = ______________

(606) 7 % = ______________

(607) 21 % = ______________

(608) 83 % = ______________

(609) 38 % = ______________

(610) 72 % = ______________

(611) 62 % = ______________

(612) 67 % = ______________

(613) 82 % = ______________

(614) 27 % = ______________

(615) 52 % = ______________

(616) 60 % = ______________

(617) 37 % = ______________

(618) 23 % = ______________

(619) 88 % = ______________

(620) 85 % = ______________

SUMMER
MATH SUCCESS

Name: ____________ Class: ________

Percent and Decimals

Convert Percent to Decimal.

(621) 24 % = ____________

(622) 40 % = ____________

(623) 43 % = ____________

(624) 25 % = ____________

(625) 37 % = ____________

(626) 77 % = ____________

(627) 73 % = ____________

(628) 8 % = ____________

(629) 89 % = ____________

(630) 46 % = ____________

(631) 74 % = ____________

(632) 47 % = ____________

(633) 27 % = ____________

(634) 100 % = ____________

(635) 13 % = ____________

(636) 19 % = ____________

(637) 23 % = ____________

(638) 86 % = ____________

(639) 42 % = ____________

(640) 32 % = ____________

SUMMER MATH SUCCESS

Name: ________________ Class: __________

Percent and Decimals

Convert Percent to Decimal.

(641) 61 % = ____________

(642) 59 % = ____________

(643) 49 % = ____________

(644) 29 % = ____________

(645) 9 % = ____________

(646) 97 % = ____________

(647) 1 % = ____________

(648) 98 % = ____________

(649) 60 % = ____________

(650) 39 % = ____________

(651) 56 % = ____________

(652) 17 % = ____________

(653) 28 % = ____________

(654) 37 % = ____________

(655) 55 % = ____________

(656) 95 % = ____________

(657) 18 % = ____________

(658) 31 % = ____________

(659) 71 % = ____________

(660) 45 % = ____________

SUMMER MATH SUCCESS

Name: ____________ Class: ________

Percent and Decimals

Convert Percent to Decimal.

(661) 10 % = ____________

(662) 31 % = ____________

(663) 83 % = ____________

(664) 16 % = ____________

(665) 61 % = ____________

(666) 25 % = ____________

(667) 41 % = ____________

(668) 14 % = ____________

(669) 33 % = ____________

(670) 38 % = ____________

(671) 52 % = ____________

(672) 82 % = ____________

(673) 57 % = ____________

(674) 65 % = ____________

(675) 91 % = ____________

(676) 15 % = ____________

(677) 17 % = ____________

(678) 40 % = ____________

(679) 76 % = ____________

(680) 49 % = ____________

SUMMER MATH SUCCESS

Name: ________________ Class: __________

Percent and Decimals

Convert Decimal to Percent.

681 0.51 = ________________

682 0.91 = ________________

683 0.57 = ________________

684 0.19 = ________________

685 0.9 = ________________

686 0.46 = ________________

687 0.01 = ________________

688 0.92 = ________________

689 0.16 = ________________

690 0.97 = ________________

691 0.22 = ________________

692 0.3 = ________________

693 0.76 = ________________

694 0.33 = ________________

695 0.69 = ________________

696 0.84 = ________________

697 0.27 = ________________

698 0.05 = ________________

699 0.35 = ________________

700 0.72 = ________________

SUMMER
MATH SUCCESS

Name: ____________ Class: ________

Percent and Decimals

Convert Decimal to Percent.

(701) 0.13 = ____________

(702) 0.9 = ____________

(703) 0.04 = ____________

(704) 0.15 = ____________

(705) 0.31 = ____________

(706) 0.7 = ____________

(707) 0.35 = ____________

(708) 0.83 = ____________

(709) 0.33 = ____________

(710) 0.26 = ____________

(711) 0.07 = ____________

(712) 0.51 = ____________

(713) 0.38 = ____________

(714) 0.96 = ____________

(715) 0.32 = ____________

(716) 0.46 = ____________

(717) 0.37 = ____________

(718) 0.85 = ____________

(719) 0.95 = ____________

(720) 0.89 = ____________

SUMMER
MATH SUCCESS

Name: ____________ Class: ________

Percent and Decimals

Convert Decimal to Percent.

(721) 0.59 = ____________

(722) 0.46 = ____________

(723) 0.33 = ____________

(724) 0.84 = ____________

(725) 0.57 = ____________

(726) 0.93 = ____________

(727) 0.22 = ____________

(728) 0.5 = ____________

(729) 0.87 = ____________

(730) 0.23 = ____________

(731) 0.47 = ____________

(732) 0.78 = ____________

(733) 0.56 = ____________

(734) 0.15 = ____________

(735) 0.97 = ____________

(736) 0.77 = ____________

(737) 0.85 = ____________

(738) 0.28 = ____________

(739) 0.48 = ____________

(740) 0.44 = ____________

SUMMER
MATH SUCCESS

Name: ________________ Class: __________

Percent and Decimals

Convert Decimal to Percent.

(741) 0.07 = ______________

(742) 0.66 = ______________

(743) 0.78 = ______________

(744) 0.06 = ______________

(745) 0.82 = ______________

(746) 0.88 = ______________

(747) 0.95 = ______________

(748) 0.56 = ______________

(749) 0.68 = ______________

(750) 0.51 = ______________

(751) 0.38 = ______________

(752) 0.19 = ______________

(753) 0.02 = ______________

(754) 0.46 = ______________

(755) 0.58 = ______________

(756) 0.48 = ______________

(757) 0.13 = ______________

(758) 0.43 = ______________

(759) 0.61 = ______________

(760) 0.83 = ______________

SUMMER MATH SUCCESS

Name: ____________ Class: ________

Percent and Decimals

Convert Decimal to Percent.

761 0.4 = ____________

762 0.82 = ____________

763 0.6 = ____________

764 0.74 = ____________

765 0.81 = ____________

766 0.36 = ____________

767 0.69 = ____________

768 0.52 = ____________

769 0.57 = ____________

770 0.48 = ____________

771 0.47 = ____________

772 0.46 = ____________

773 0.56 = ____________

774 0.78 = ____________

775 0.76 = ____________

776 0.05 = ____________

777 0.27 = ____________

778 0.95 = ____________

779 0.19 = ____________

780 0.72 = ____________

SUMMER
MATH SUCCESS

Name: ____________ Class: ________

Percent - Advanced

Calculate the given percent of each value.

(781) 0.8% of 146 = ☐

(782) 1.3% of ☐ = 0.039

(783) 0.8% of 57 = ☐

(784) ☐ of 373 = 16.039

(785) 0.3% of ☐ = 0.117

(786) 2.4% of ☐ = 21.432

(787) 1.2% of 59 = ☐

(788) ☐ of 208 = 1.664

(789) 5.9% of 20 = ☐

(790) ☐ of 482 = 22.654

(791) ☐ of 343 = 1.029

(792) 5.6% of ☐ = 33.768

(793) 1.5% of 104 = ☐

(794) 0.8% of 1 = ☐

(795) ☐ of 755 = 71.725

(796) 5.6% of ☐ = 3.64

(797) 0.1% of 66 = ☐

(798) ☐ of 772 = 6.176

(799) ☐ of 13 = 0.533

(800) ☐ of 322 = 18.676

SUMMER
MATH SUCCESS

Name: ____________ Class: ________

Percent - Advanced

Calculate the given percent of each value.

(801) 6.6% of ☐ = 4.752

(802) ☐ of 197 = 7.88

(803) ☐ of 678 = 6.102

(804) 9.7% of ☐ = 6.208

(805) 5.7% of ☐ = 0.342

(806) ☐ of 6 = 0.114

(807) ☐ of 2 = 0.004

(808) 6.1% of 897 = ☐

(809) 0.5% of ☐ = 0.015

(810) 0.8% of ☐ = 0.072

(811) ☐ of 997 = 85.742

(812) 5.3% of ☐ = 0.053

(813) ☐ of 226 = 7.91

(814) ☐ of 60 = 2.76

(815) ☐ of 89 = 6.497

(816) 0.5% of 70 = ☐

(817) 3.2% of 332 = ☐

(818) 0.8% of ☐ = 5.48

(819) 7.4% of ☐ = 38.332

(820) 0.6% of ☐ = 5.55

SUMMER MATH SUCCESS

Name: ____________ Class: ________

Percent - Advanced

Calculate the given percent of each value.

(821) ☐ of 6 = 0.03

(822) 0.8% of 272 = ☐

(823) ☐ of 17 = 0.731

(824) 6.0% of ☐ = 0.3

(825) ☐ of 968 = 8.712

(826) 2.9% of ☐ = 8.381

(827) 3.8% of ☐ = 0.304

(828) ☐ of 6 = 0.534

(829) ☐ of 333 = 28.305

(830) 9.1% of ☐ = 0.728

(831) ☐ of 7 = 0.063

(832) 3.9% of ☐ = 0.078

(833) 8.4% of ☐ = 53.004

(834) ☐ of 59 = 4.602

(835) 0.3% of ☐ = 1.713

(836) 6.6% of ☐ = 6.336

(837) 4.3% of ☐ = 2.709

(838) 0.8% of ☐ = 0.8

(839) 7.5% of 951 = ☐

(840) 0.3% of 26 = ☐

SUMMER
MATH SUCCESS

Name: ____________ Class: ________

Percent - Advanced

Calculate the given percent of each value.

(841) ☐ of 56 = 3.808

(842) 0.3% of 253 = ☐

(843) 0.3% of ☐ = 0.57

(844) 3.5% of ☐ = 23.1

(845) 3.0% of 994 = ☐

(846) 9.0% of ☐ = 0.27

(847) ☐ of 67 = 0.402

(848) 0.3% of ☐ = 0.015

(849) 2.7% of ☐ = 0.081

(850) 1.1% of 942 = ☐

(851) 0.9% of 32 = ☐

(852) ☐ of 4 = 0.028

(853) 0.8% of ☐ = 1.36

(854) ☐ of 41 = 3.69

(855) ☐ of 5 = 0.415

(856) 0.4% of ☐ = 0.144

(857) 4.0% of 95 = ☐

(858) ☐ of 3 = 0.183

(859) ☐ of 8 = 0.168

(860) 0.4% of 2 = ☐

SUMMER
MATH SUCCESS

Name: ______________ Class: __________

Percent - Advanced

Calculate the given percent of each value.

(861) 0.3% of ☐ = 0.126

(862) 9.7% of 61 = ☐

(863) ☐ of 22 = 0.022

(864) 0.8% of ☐ = 0.064

(865) 5.9% of 49 = ☐

(866) ☐ of 1 = 0.003

(867) 0.5% of 180 = ☐

(868) 2.7% of 1 = ☐

(869) ☐ of 97 = 4.753

(870) ☐ of 3 = 0.003

(871) ☐ of 4 = 0.356

(872) ☐ of 976 = 8.784

(873) 8.1% of 190 = ☐

(874) ☐ of 13 = 0.026

(875) ☐ of 4 = 0.02

(876) ☐ of 574 = 3.444

(877) ☐ of 576 = 42.048

(878) 3.8% of ☐ = 0.266

(879) 2.4% of ☐ = 0.12

(880) 0.8% of ☐ = 0.384

SUMMER
MATH SUCCESS

Name: ____________ Class: ________

Percent - Advanced

Calculate the given percent of each value.

881) 4.3% of ☐ = 18.146

882) 0.5% of 942 = ☐

883) ☐ of 7 = 0.063

884) 7.9% of 84 = ☐

885) 0.4% of ☐ = 0.012

886) 4.4% of 9 = ☐

887) 5.8% of ☐ = 10.208

888) 0.6% of ☐ = 0.138

889) 7.0% of 889 = ☐

890) 0.7% of ☐ = 0.672

891) 0.4% of ☐ = 0.912

892) ☐ of 954 = 71.55

893) 4.1% of ☐ = 0.041

894) 0.6% of ☐ = 0.018

895) 1.5% of ☐ = 0.405

896) ☐ of 665 = 36.575

897) 0.1% of ☐ = 0.004

898) 5.2% of ☐ = 22.88

899) 7.9% of ☐ = 50.007

900) ☐ of 261 = 0.261

SUMMER MATH SUCCESS

Name: ____________ Class: ________

Percent - Advanced

Calculate the given percent of each value.

(901) 0.2% of 915 = ☐

(902) ☐ of 74 = 0.444

(903) 0.8% of 58 = ☐

(904) ☐ of 33 = 0.561

(905) 1.0% of 8 = ☐

(906) ☐ of 394 = 2.364

(907) ☐ of 178 = 11.214

(908) 4.5% of ☐ = 2.475

(909) 9.2% of 885 = ☐

(910) ☐ of 316 = 0.948

(911) ☐ of 392 = 16.072

(912) 0.5% of ☐ = 0.015

(913) ☐ of 553 = 34.839

(914) 6.7% of ☐ = 1.474

(915) ☐ of 405 = 19.44

(916) 9.8% of ☐ = 0.588

(917) ☐ of 129 = 12.642

(918) 0.2% of ☐ = 1.988

(919) ☐ of 63 = 0.378

(920) 0.5% of ☐ = 2.09

SUMMER
MATH SUCCESS

Name: ________ Class: ________

Percent - Advanced

Calculate the given percent of each value.

(921) 0.4% of ☐ = 0.008

(922) 5.8% of ☐ = 56.202

(923) ☐ of 810 = 62.37

(924) 0.3% of ☐ = 0.009

(925) 0.8% of 647 = ☐

(926) 0.7% of ☐ = 0.014

(927) 2.5% of ☐ = 0.025

(928) 4.0% of 8 = ☐

(929) 0.8% of 8 = ☐

(930) ☐ of 147 = 13.23

(931) ☐ of 58 = 0.232

(932) 0.4% of ☐ = 0.004

(933) ☐ of 25 = 0.225

(934) 5.6% of ☐ = 4.032

(935) 2.5% of ☐ = 20.125

(936) ☐ of 76 = 4.94

(937) ☐ of 224 = 12.992

(938) 6.4% of 589 = ☐

(939) ☐ of 78 = 5.07

(940) 2.6% of 8 = ☐

SUMMER
MATH SUCCESS

Name: ____________ Class: ________

Percent - Advanced

Calculate the given percent of each value.

(941) ☐ of 37 = 3.367

(942) ☐ of 699 = 2.097

(943) ☐ of 281 = 21.356

(944) 8.6% of 38 = ☐

(945) ☐ of 515 = 2.06

(946) 6.5% of ☐ = 28.47

(947) ☐ of 460 = 10.12

(948) 4.3% of ☐ = 0.301

(949) 4.9% of 455 = ☐

(950) ☐ of 30 = 1.65

(951) 0.9% of ☐ = 0.054

(952) 7.0% of ☐ = 4.2

(953) 0.5% of 78 = ☐

(954) ☐ of 453 = 27.633

(955) ☐ of 953 = 32.402

(956) ☐ of 497 = 3.479

(957) 4.0% of 5 = ☐

(958) 3.2% of ☐ = 18.016

(959) 0.6% of 3 = ☐

(960) 0.3% of 5 = ☐

SUMMER MATH SUCCESS

Name: ____________ Class: ________

Percent - Advanced

Calculate the given percent of each value.

961 ☐ of 728 = 6.552

962 9.6% of 897 = ☐

963 ☐ of 5 = 0.035

964 ☐ of 3 = 0.003

965 ☐ of 6 = 0.012

966 4.0% of ☐ = 0.2

967 ☐ of 5 = 0.465

968 0.5% of ☐ = 0.01

969 ☐ of 97 = 4.074

970 0.9% of 157 = ☐

971 ☐ of 9 = 0.648

972 7.0% of 28 = ☐

973 ☐ of 56 = 3.808

974 0.7% of ☐ = 0.574

975 ☐ of 2 = 0.004

976 8.9% of ☐ = 0.445

977 7.2% of 22 = ☐

978 ☐ of 817 = 1.634

979 ☐ of 44 = 2.992

980 5.9% of 88 = ☐

SUMMER MATH SUCCESS

Name: ____________ Class: ________

Ratio Conversions

Provide the conversions for each ratio (Part to Part).

981

	Ratio	Fraction	Percent	Decimal
a.	1:2			
b.	3:8			
c.	5:6			
d.	1:6			
e.	1:1			
f.	1:5			
g.	4:7			
h.	1:4			
i.	5:7			
j.	3:9			
k.	7:10			
l.	1:8			
m.	3:7			

SUMMER MATH SUCCESS

Name: ____________ Class: ________

Ratio Conversions

Provide the conversions for each ratio (Part to Part).

982

	Ratio	Fraction	Percent	Decimal
a.	8:9			
b.	9:10			
c.	4:6			
d.	1:8			
e.	1:6			
f.	3:3			
g.	1:4			
h.	3:5			
i.	6:7			
j.	4:9			
k.	6:9			
l.	2:5			
m.	4:7			

SUMMER MATH SUCCESS

Name: ____________ Class: ________

Ratio Conversions

Provide the conversions for each ratio (Part to Part).

983

	Ratio	Fraction	Percent	Decimal
a.	1:1			
b.	1:2			
c.	8:10			
d.	4:8			
e.	2:8			
f.	1:4			
g.	4:6			
h.	5:8			
i.	2:3			
j.	4:10			
k.	3:7			
l.	7:10			
m.	5:9			

SUMMER MATH SUCCESS

Name: ____________ Class: ________

Ratio Conversions

Provide the conversions for each ratio (Part to Part).

984

	Ratio	Fraction	Percent	Decimal
a.				0.5
b.			20%	
c.		3/4		
d.		3/5		
e.				0.625
f.			100%	
g.		2/3		
h.			14.3%	
i.				0.6
j.	1:3			
k.			77.8%	
l.			40%	
m.		4/9		

SUMMER MATH SUCCESS

Name: ____________ Class: ________

Ratio Conversions

Provide the conversions for each ratio (Part to Part).

985

	Ratio	Fraction	Percent	Decimal
a.	7:10			
b.			60%	
c.	1:3			
d.			88.9%	
e.		4/10		
f.				0.4
g.		4/5		
h.			30%	
i.				0.833
j.			100%	
k.	5:8			
l.				0.667
m.		4/9		

SUMMER MATH SUCCESS

Name: ________________ Class: __________

Ratio Conversions

Provide the conversions for each ratio (Part to Part).

986

	Ratio	Fraction	Percent	Decimal
a.	1:2			
b.			66.7%	
c.		6/7		
d.				0.5
e.		1/1		
f.			60%	
g.		6/8		
h.	1:6			
i.		2/3		
j.			33.3%	
k.				0.5
l.	1:4			
m.	3:4			

SUMMER MATH SUCCESS

Name: ____________ Class: ________

Ratio Conversions

Provide the conversions for each ratio (Part to Part).

987

	Ratio	Fraction	Percent	Decimal
a.				1
b.	1:2			
c.				0.286
d.		3/10		
e.			75%	
f.			57.1%	
g.			25%	
h.	1:4			
i.		1/5		
j.			40%	
k.	1:3			
l.		4/5		
m.	3:6			

SUMMER MATH SUCCESS

Name: ____________ Class: ________

Cartesian Coordinates

Fill in as indicated.

988

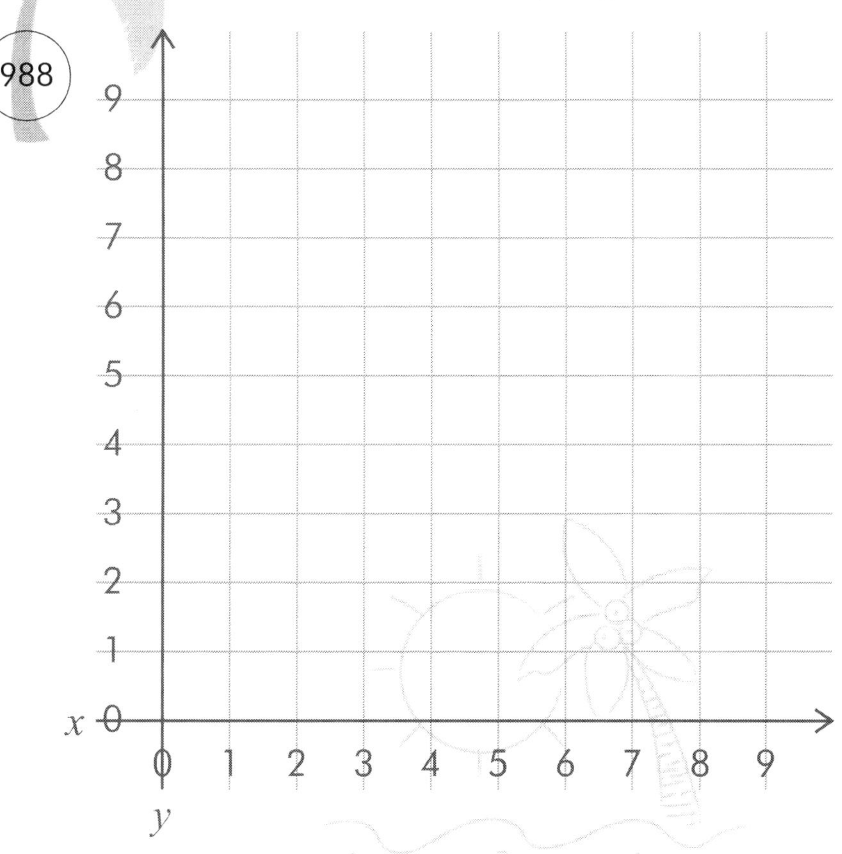

A = (4, 5)

B = (6, 0)

C = (1, 7)

D = (6, 4)

E = (7, 1)

F = (6, 1)

G = (2, 7)

H = (3, 1)

I = (7, 5)

J = (2, 0)

SUMMER
MATH SUCCESS

Name: ____________ Class: ________

Cartesian Coordinates
Fill in as indicated.

989

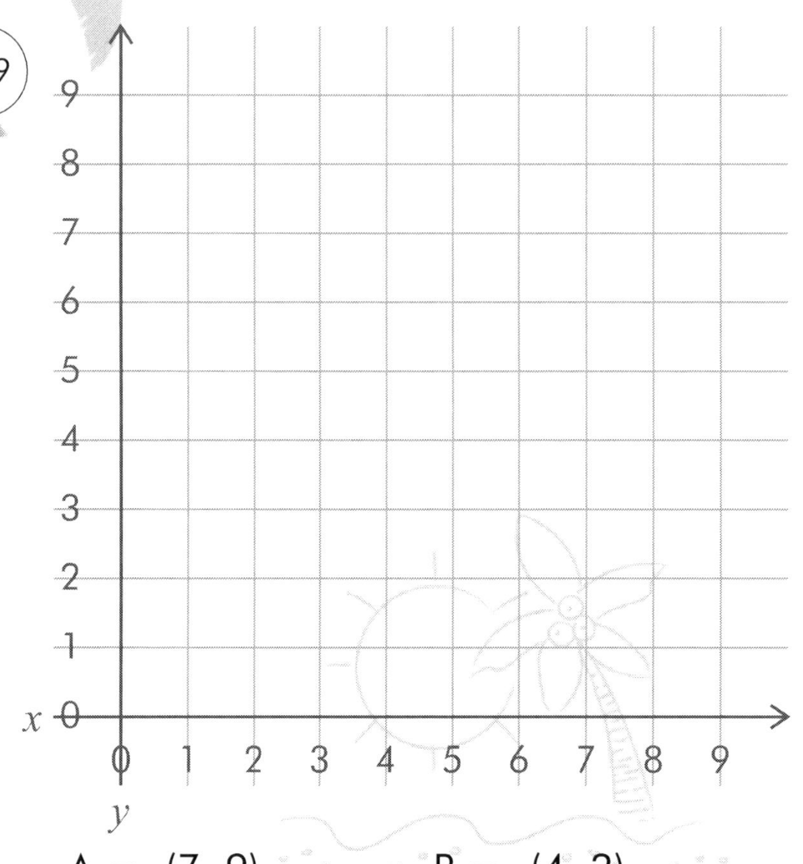

A = (7, 9) B = (4, 3)

C = (9, 3) D = (4, 9)

E = (5, 5) F = (5, 8)

G = (5, 2) H = (0, 5)

I = (4, 0) J = (3, 8)

SUMMER
MATH SUCCESS

Name: ____________ Class: ________

Cartesian Coordinates
Fill in as indicated.

990

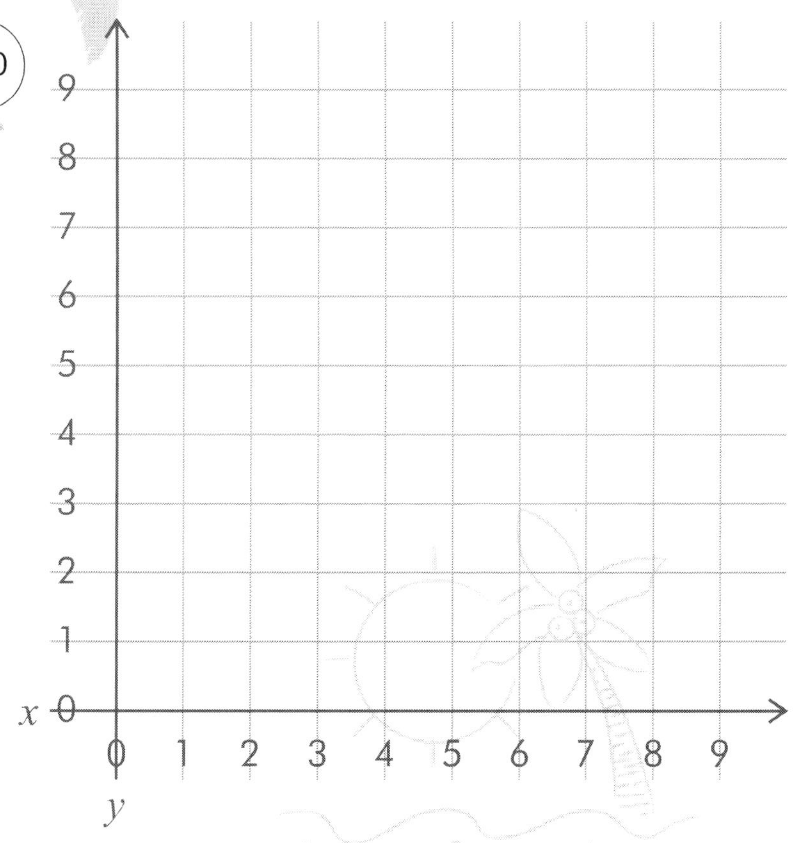

A = (2, 2) B = (1, 5)

C = (6, 2) D = (4, 9)

E = (6, 8) F = (2, 6)

G = (2, 1) H = (3, 2)

I = (4, 3) J = (7, 6)

SUMMER MATH SUCCESS

Name: ____________ Class: ________

Cartesian Coordinates

Fill in as indicated.

991

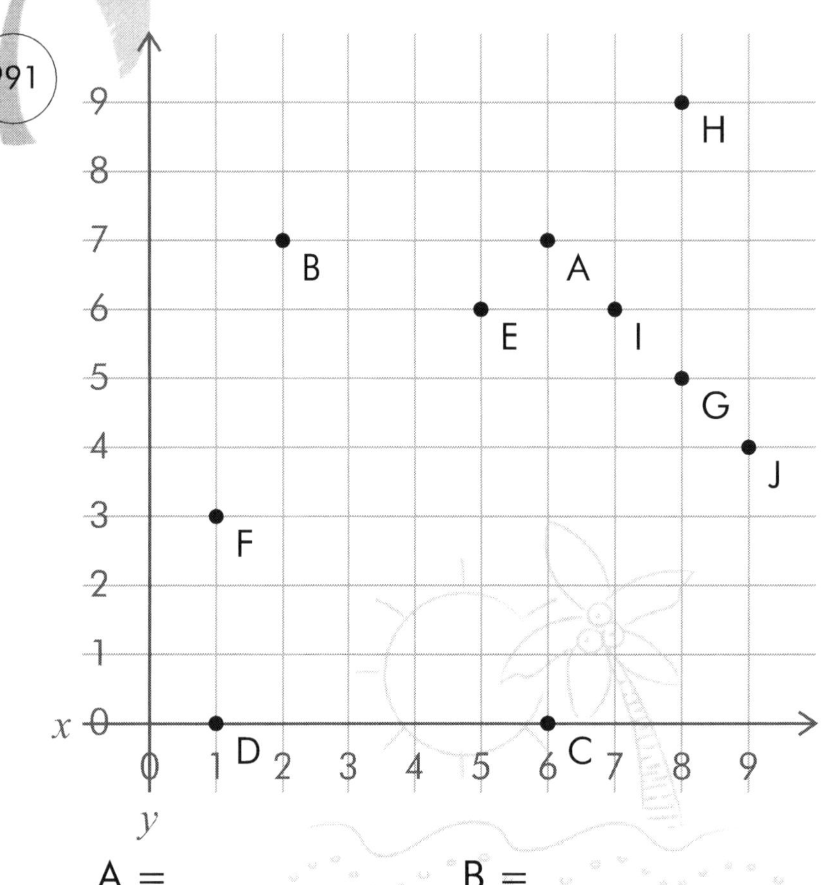

A = ____________ B = ____________

C = ____________ D = ____________

E = ____________ F = ____________

G = ____________ H = ____________

I = ____________ J = ____________

SUMMER
MATH SUCCESS

Name: ____________ Class: ________

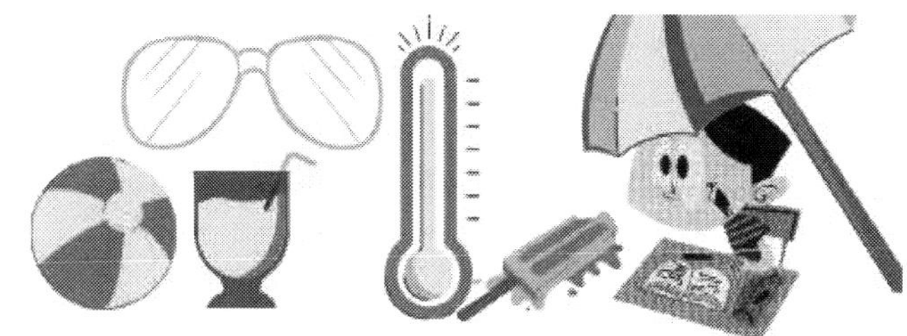

Cartesian Coordinates
Fill in as indicated.

992

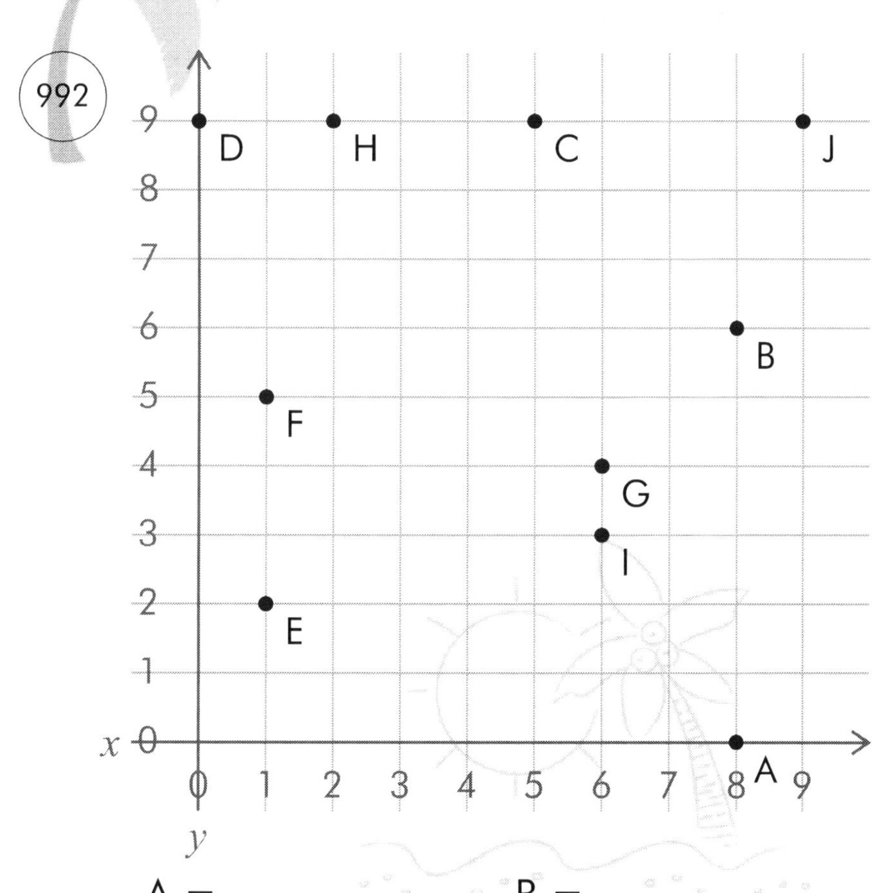

A = ____________ B = ____________

C = ____________ D = ____________

E = ____________ F = ____________

G = ____________ H = ____________

I = ____________ J = ____________

SUMMER MATH SUCCESS

Name: ____________________ Class: ___________

Cartesian Coordinates

Fill in as indicated.

993

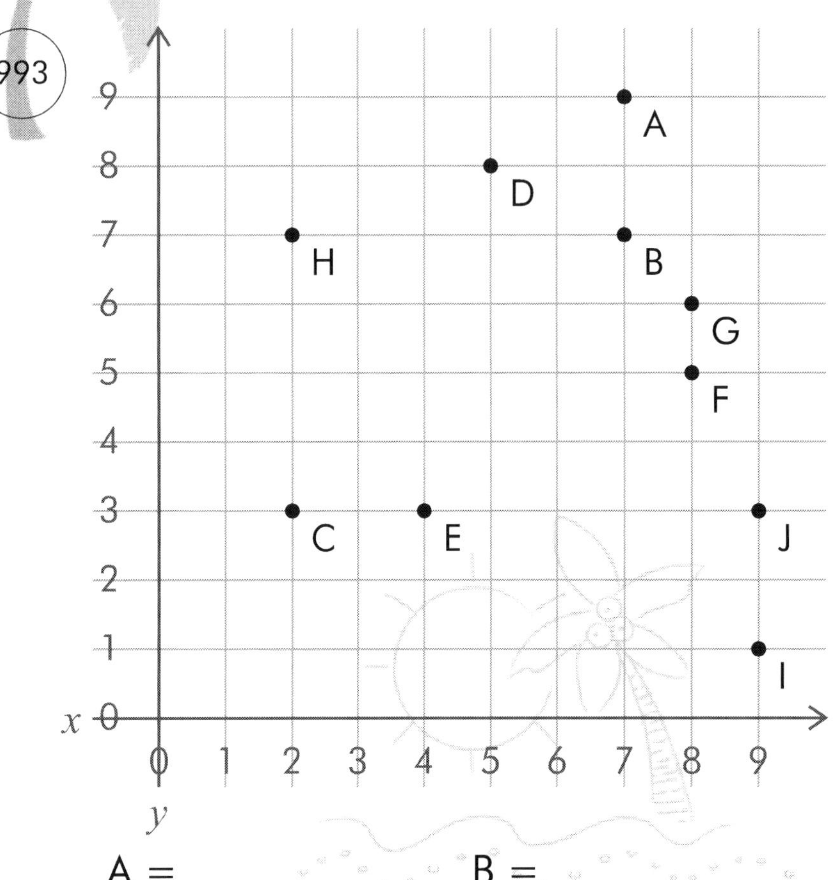

A = ______________ B = ______________

C = ______________ D = ______________

E = ______________ F = ______________

G = ______________ H = ______________

I = ______________ J = ______________

Name: ____________ Class: ________

Cartesian Coordinates With Four Quadrants

Fill in as indicated.

994

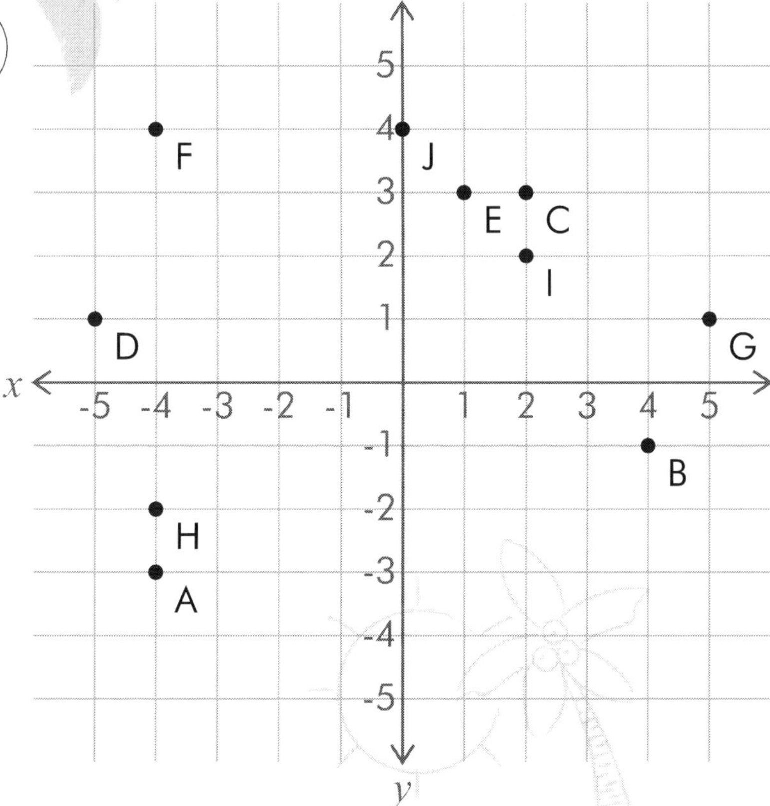

A = ____________ B = ____________

C = ____________ D = ____________

E = ____________ F = ____________

G = ____________ H = ____________

I = ____________ J = ____________

SUMMER MATH SUCCESS

Name: ______________ Class: __________

Cartesian Coordinates With Four Quadrants

Fill in as indicated.

995

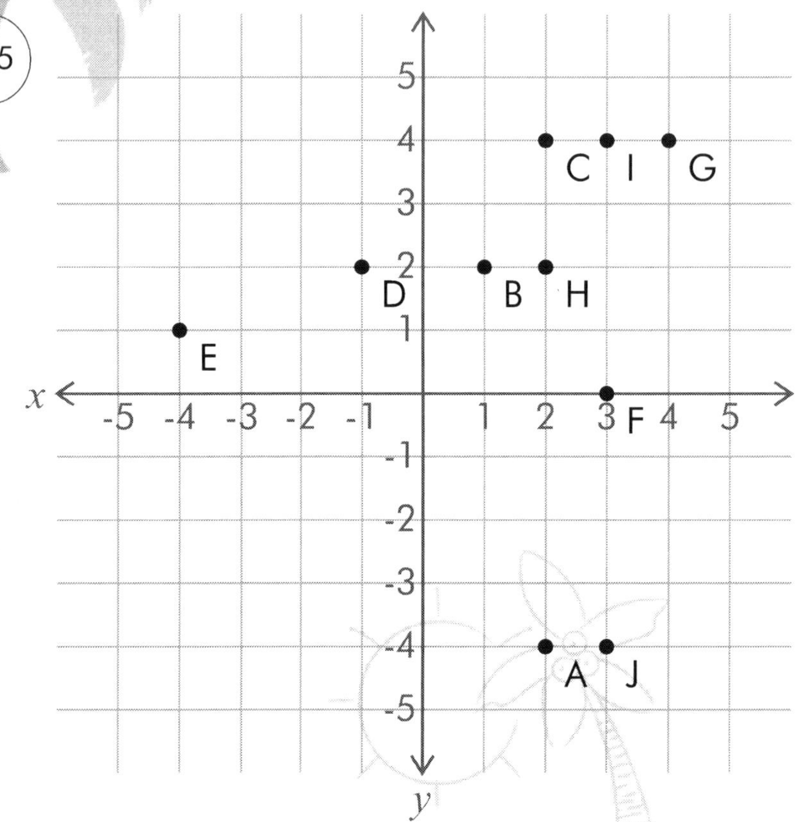

A = ______________ B = ______________

C = ______________ D = ______________

E = ______________ F = ______________

G = ______________ H = ______________

I = ______________ J = ______________

SUMMER MATH SUCCESS

Name: ____________ Class: ________

Cartesian Coordinates With Four Quadrants

Fill in as indicated.

996

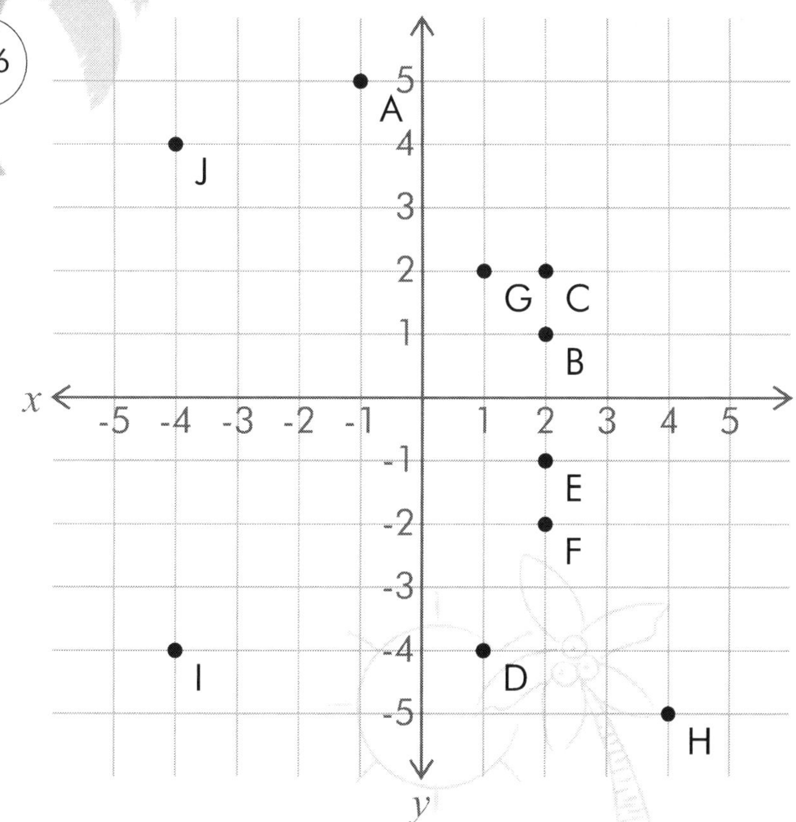

A = ____________ B = ____________

C = ____________ D = ____________

E = ____________ F = ____________

G = ____________ H = ____________

I = ____________ J = ____________

SUMMER MATH SUCCESS

Name: ____________ Class: ____________

Cartesian Coordinates With Four Quadrants

Fill in as indicated.

997

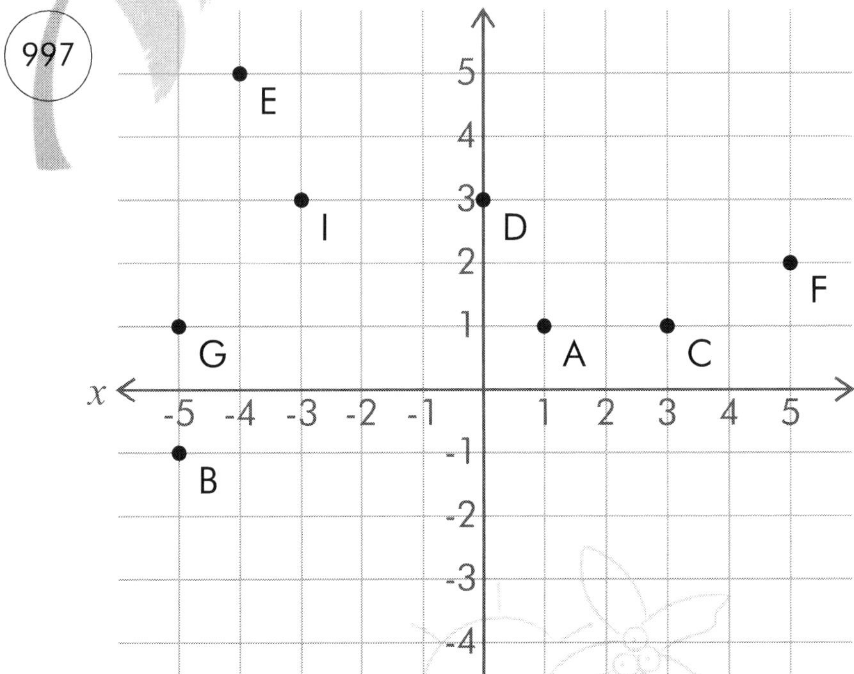

A = ____________ B = ____________

C = ____________ D = ____________

E = ____________ F = ____________

G = ____________ H = ____________

I = ____________ J = ____________

SUMMER
MATH SUCCESS

Name: ____________________ Class: __________

Cartesian Coordinates With Four Quadrants

Fill in as indicated.

998

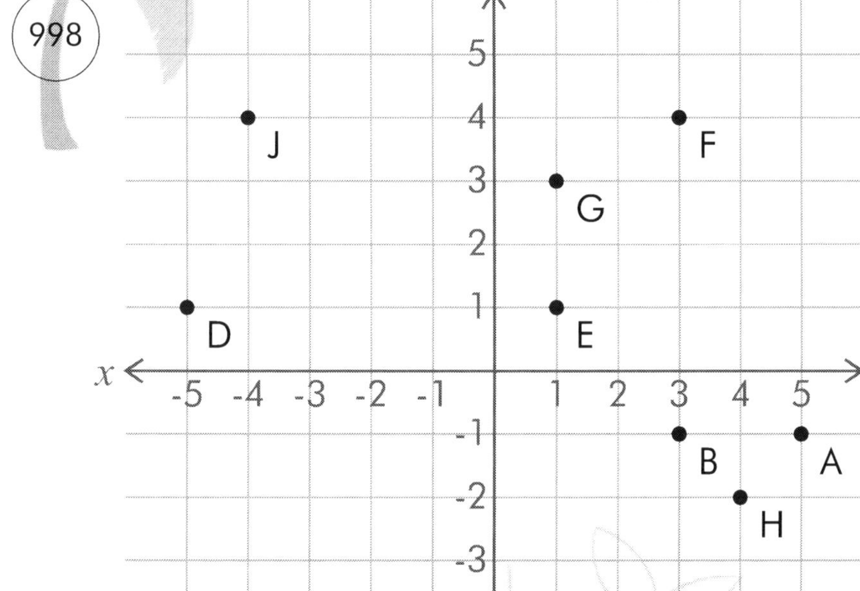

A = ______________ B = ______________

C = ______________ D = ______________

E = ______________ F = ______________

G = ______________ H = ______________

I = ______________ J = ______________

Name: ________________ Class: __________

Cartesian Coordinates With Four Quadrants

Fill in as indicated.

999

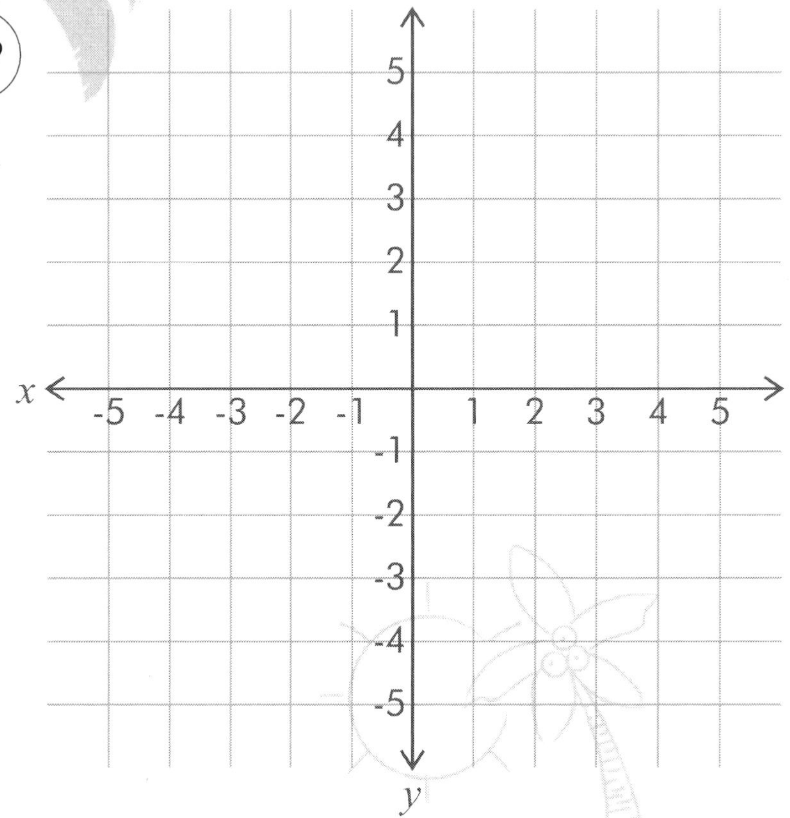

A = (5, 2) B = (0, -5)

C = (-3, 5) D = (5, -3)

E = (-4, -5) F = (5, -1)

G = (3, 0) H = (2, 2)

I = (1, -2) J = (2, 0)

Name: ______________ Class: __________

Cartesian Coordinates With Four Quadrants

Fill in as indicated.

1000

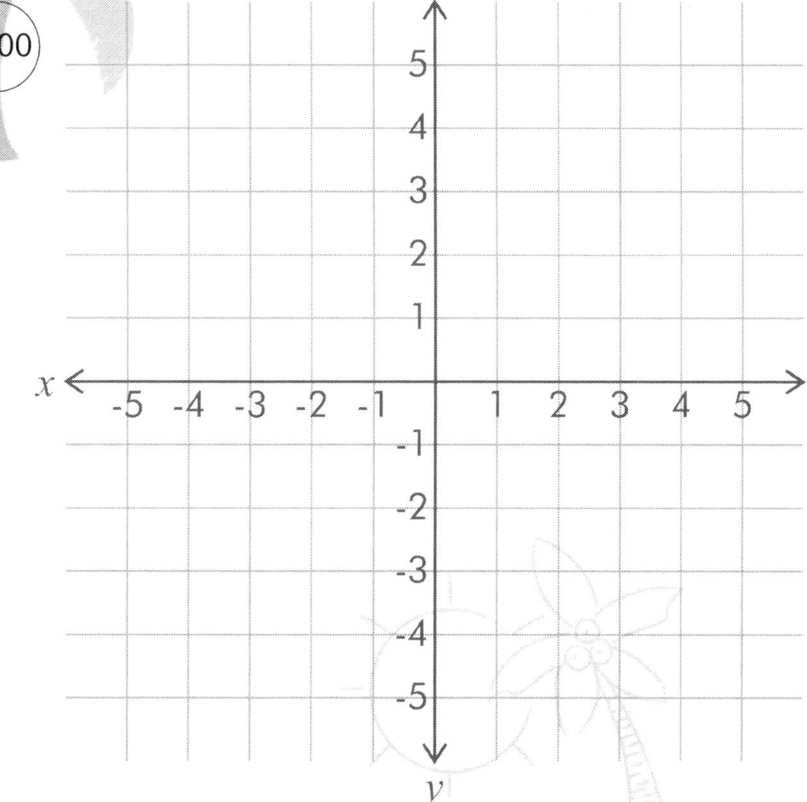

A = (-1, -2) B = (4, -3)

C = (-5, -5) D = (2, 2)

E = (-3, -4) F = (1, -2)

G = (-4, -3) H = (4, 3)

I = (-3, -5) J = (-3, 4)

SUMMER MATH SUCCESS

Name: ________________ Class: __________

Cartesian Coordinates With Four Quadrants

Fill in as indicated.

1001

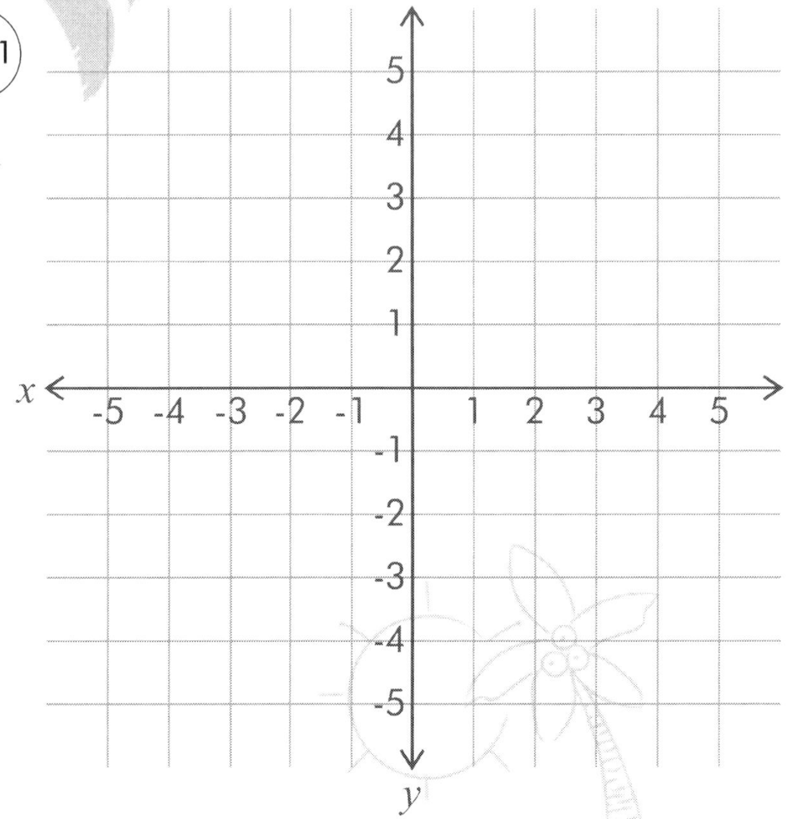

A = (0, 0) B = (2, -2)

C = (-4, -4) D = (-5, -3)

E = (2, 0) F = (0, 4)

G = (-4, 0) H = (-3, -3)

I = (-4, -5) J = (5, 5)

SUMMER MATH SUCCESS

Name: ____________ Class: __________

Cartesian Coordinates With Four Quadrants

Fill in as indicated.

1002

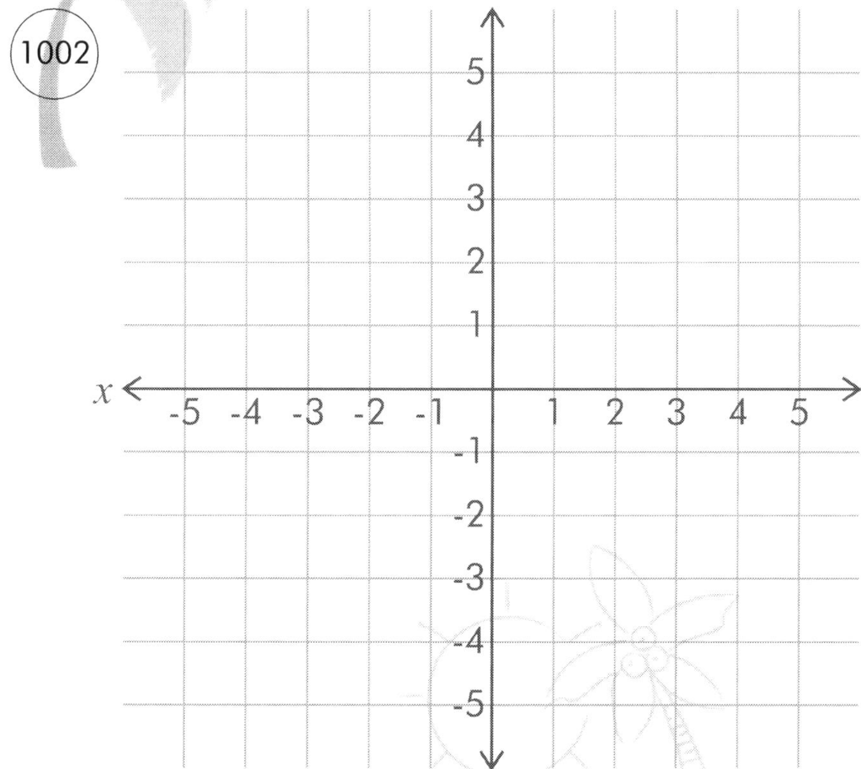

A = (0, 0) B = (4, 3)

C = (4, 0) D = (-1, -1)

E = (4, 4) F = (-4, 1)

G = (-4, 4) H = (5, 4)

I = (1, 1) J = (-5, 5)

SUMMER
MATH SUCCESS

Name: ____________ Class: ________

Cartesian Coordinates With Four Quadrants

Fill in as indicated.

1003

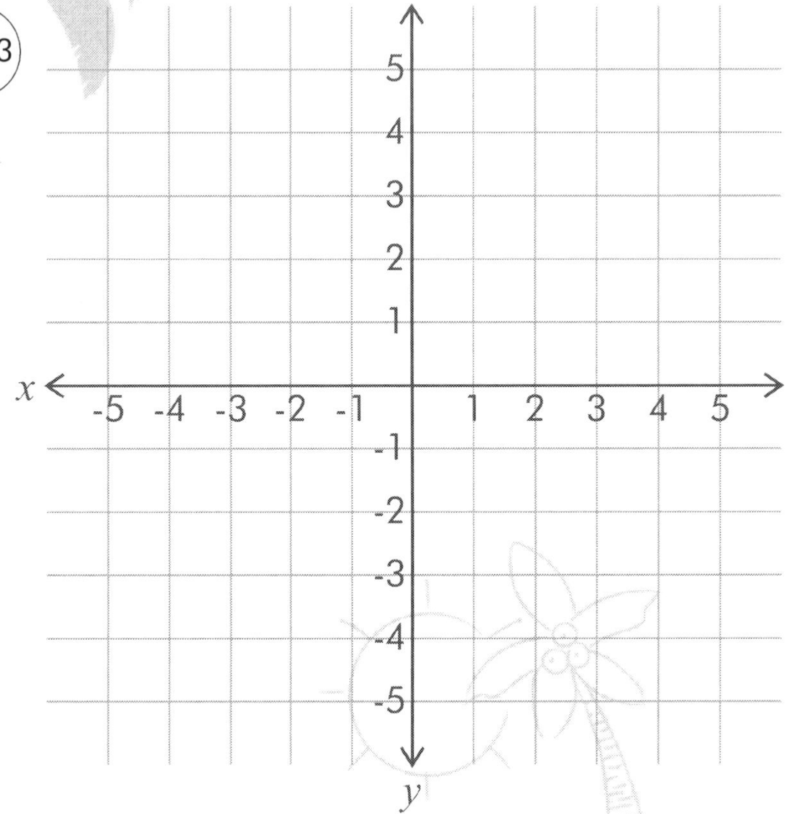

A = (5, 0) B = (5, 3)

C = (2, 2) D = (-4, 1)

E = (-5, 2) F = (2, -4)

G = (-5, -3) H = (-2, -5)

I = (2, 5) J = (0, 2)

SUMMER MATH SUCCESS

Name: ____________________ Class: __________

Plot Lines

Plot and draw the lines.

1004

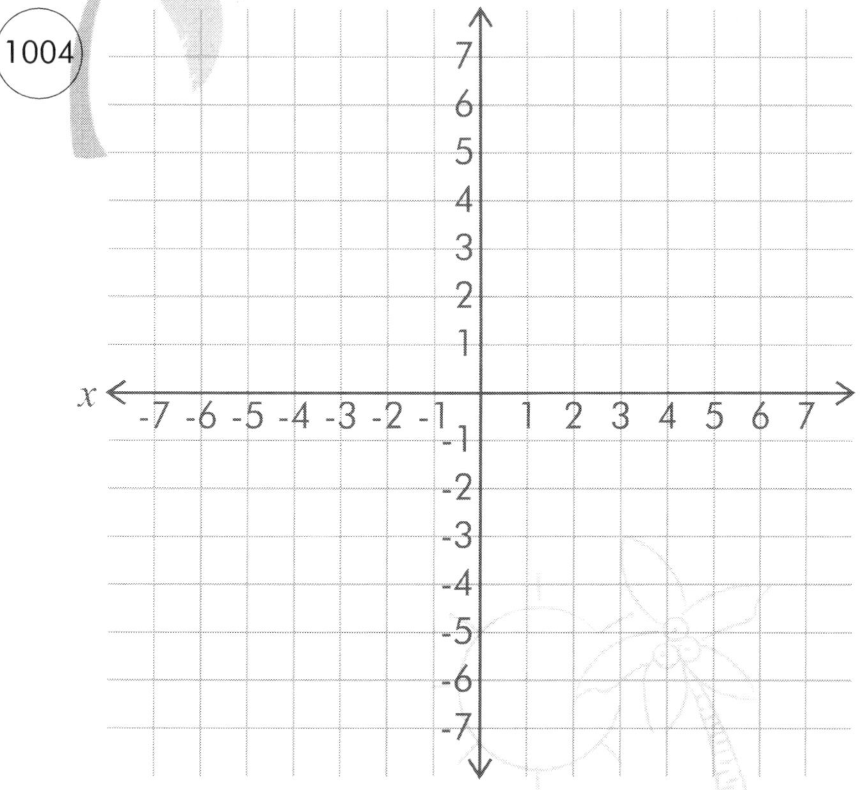

A = (6, 2)　　B = (-2, 6)

C = (0, 5)　　D = (2, 4)

E = (-4, 7)　　F = (4, 3)

SUMMER MATH SUCCESS

Name: ________________ Class: __________

Plot Lines

Plot and draw the lines.

1005

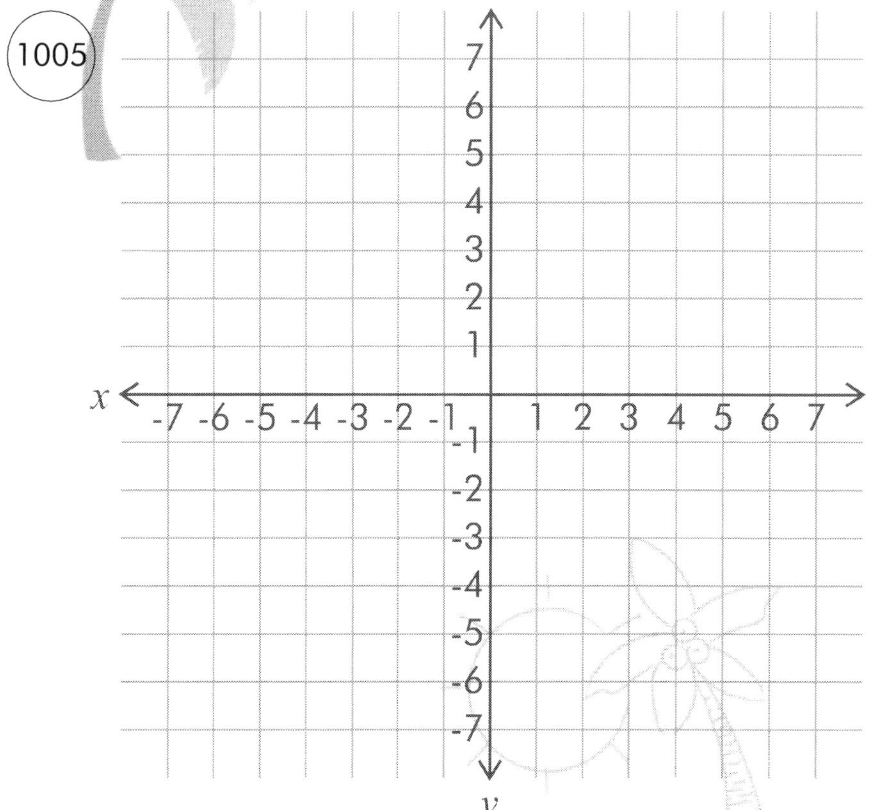

A = (1, 4) B = (0, 5)

C = (3, 2) D = (7, -2)

E = (-2, 7) F = (2, 3)

SUMMER MATH SUCCESS

Name: ____________ Class: ________

Plot Lines

Plot and draw the lines.

1006

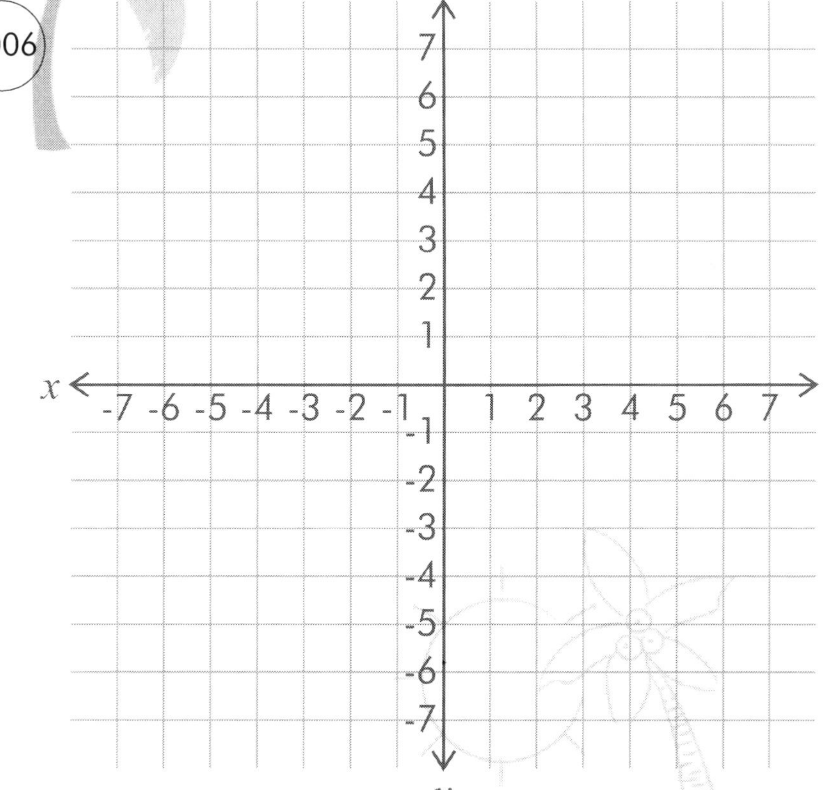

A = (0, -2) B = (-6, -2)

C = (-3, -2) D = (6, -2)

E = (3, -2) F = (-7, -2)

SUMMER
MATH SUCCESS

Name: ____________ Class: ________

Plot Lines

Plot and draw the lines.

1007

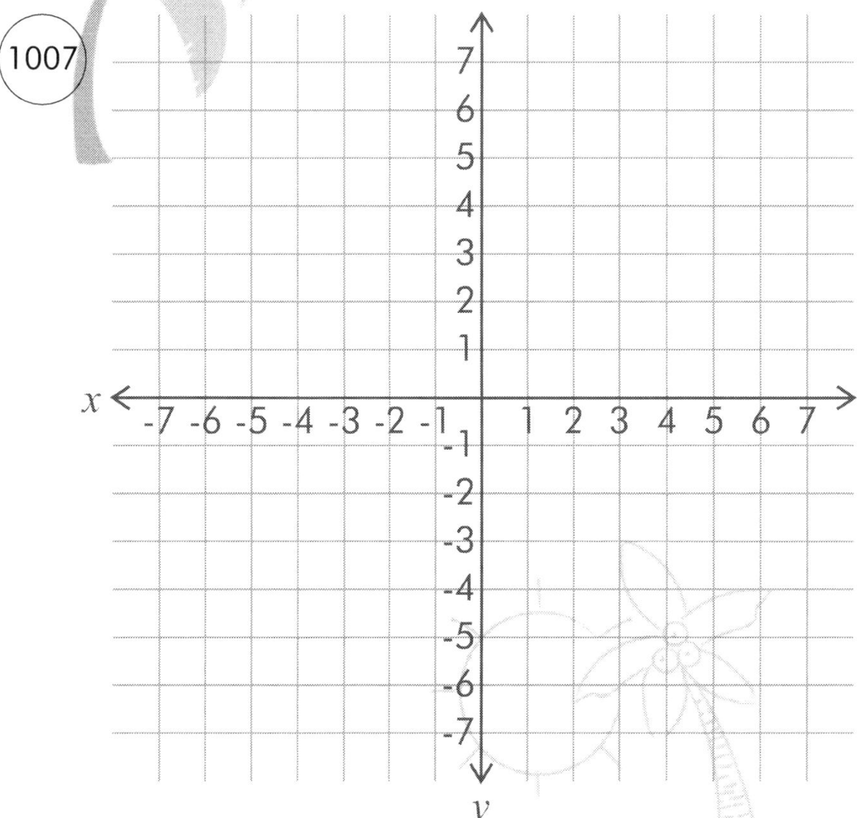

A = (1, 2) B = (4, 5)

C = (5, 6) D = (-3, -2)

E = (-6, -5) F = (0, 1)

SUMMER MATH SUCCESS

Name: ____________ Class: ________

Plot Lines

Plot and draw the lines.

1008

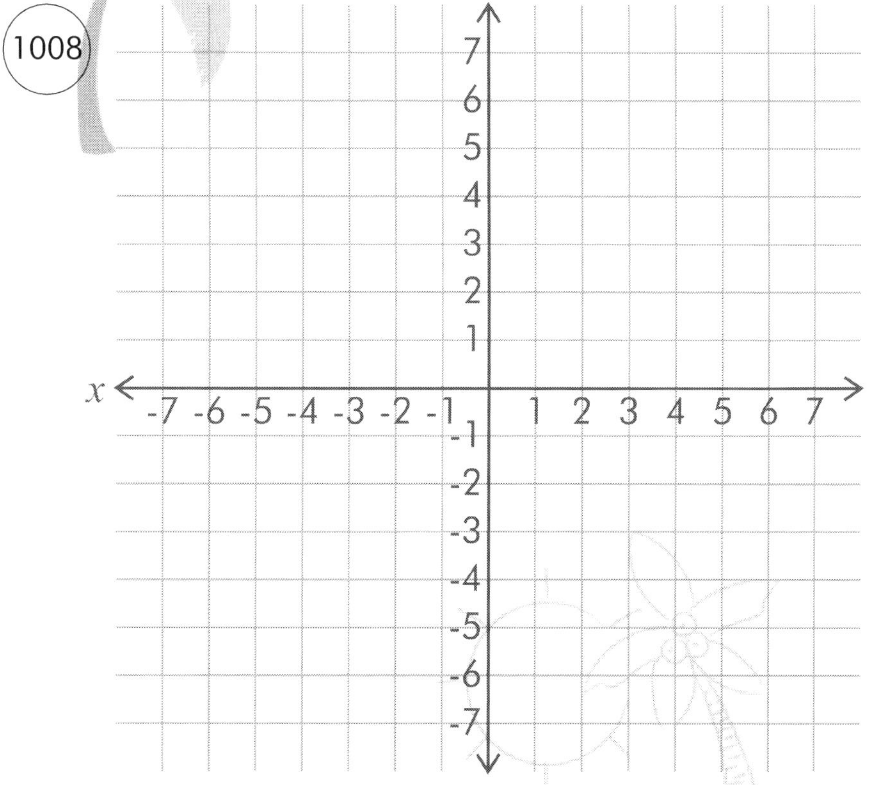

A = (7, -6) B = (-3, -6)

C = (4, -6) D = (6, -6)

E = (5, -6) F = (1, -6)

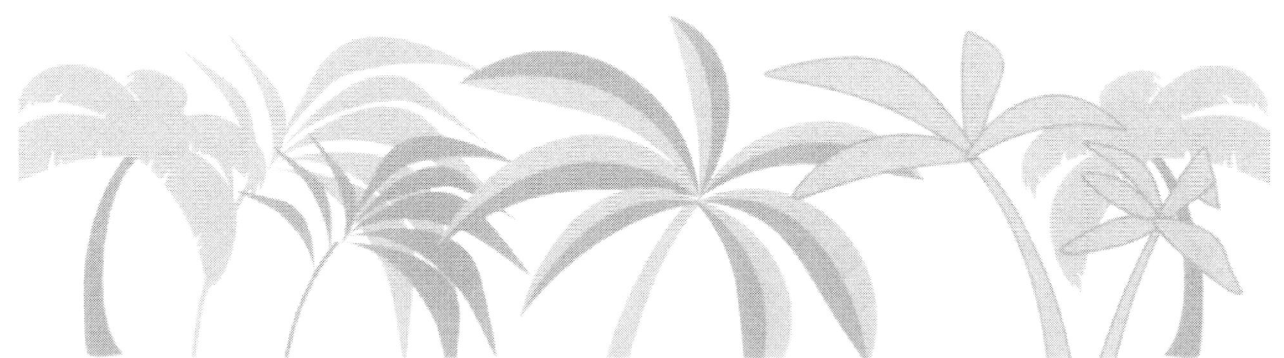

SUMMER MATH SUCCESS

Name: ________________ Class: __________

Plot Lines

Plot and draw the lines.

1009

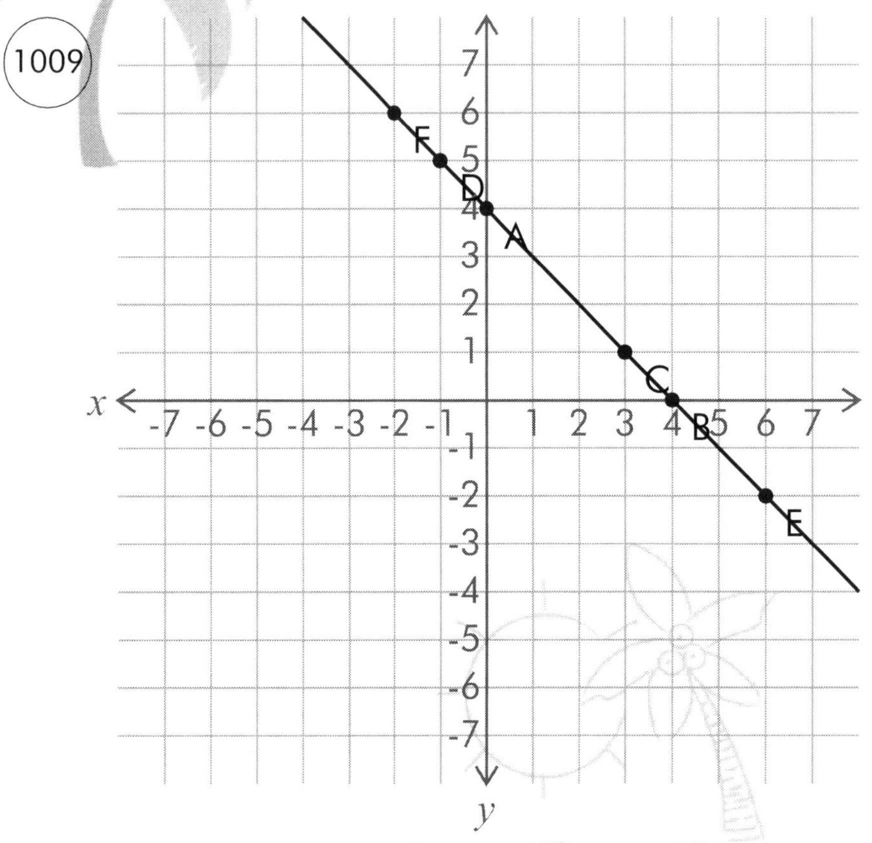

A = ______________ B = ______________

C = ______________ D = ______________

E = ______________ F = ______________

SUMMER
MATH SUCCESS

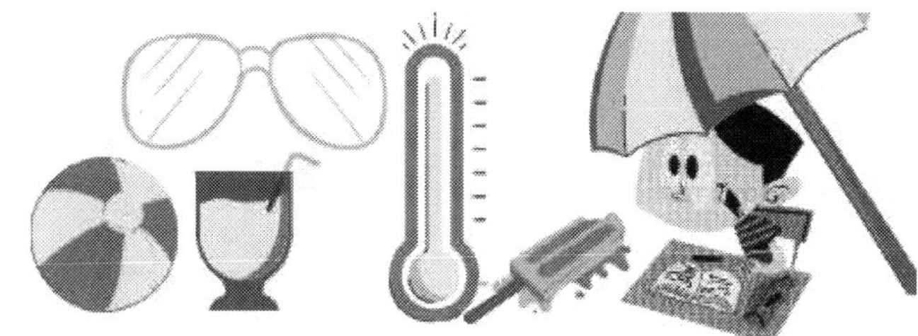

Name: ________________ Class: __________

Plot Lines

Plot and draw the lines.

1010

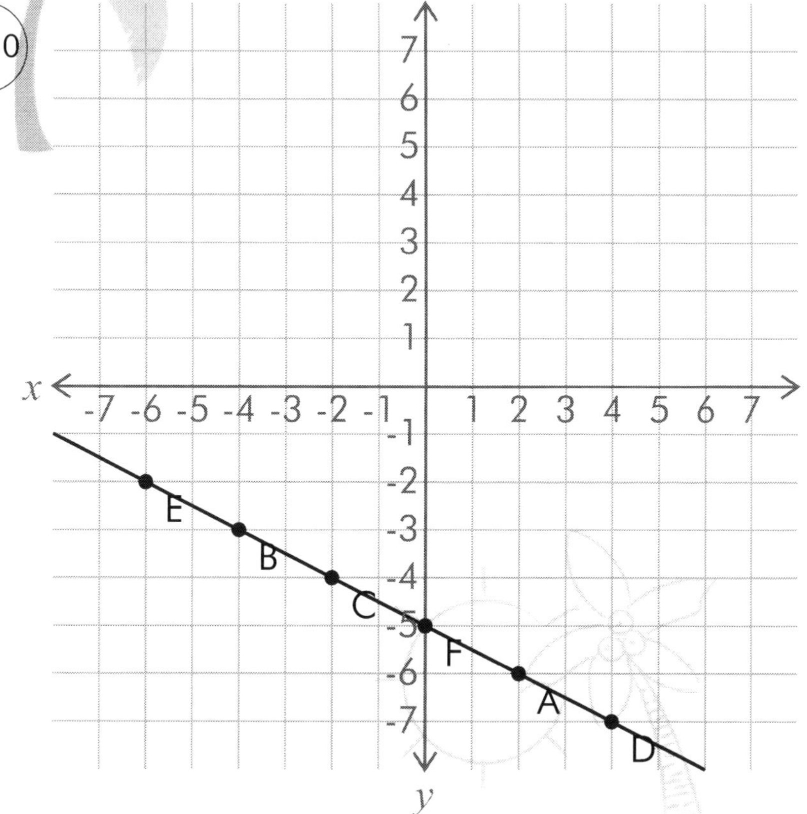

A = ______________ B = ______________

C = ______________ D = ______________

E = ______________ F = ______________

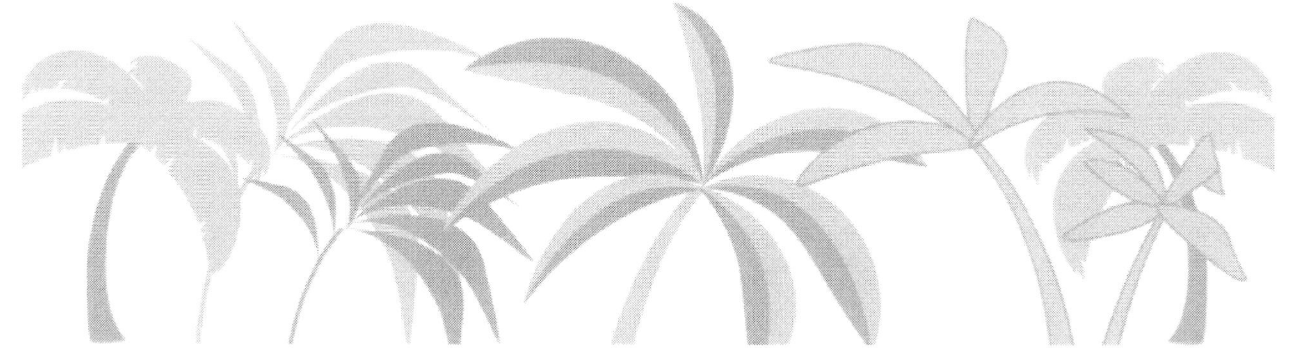

Name: ____________________ Class: ___________

Plot Lines

Plot and draw the lines.

1011

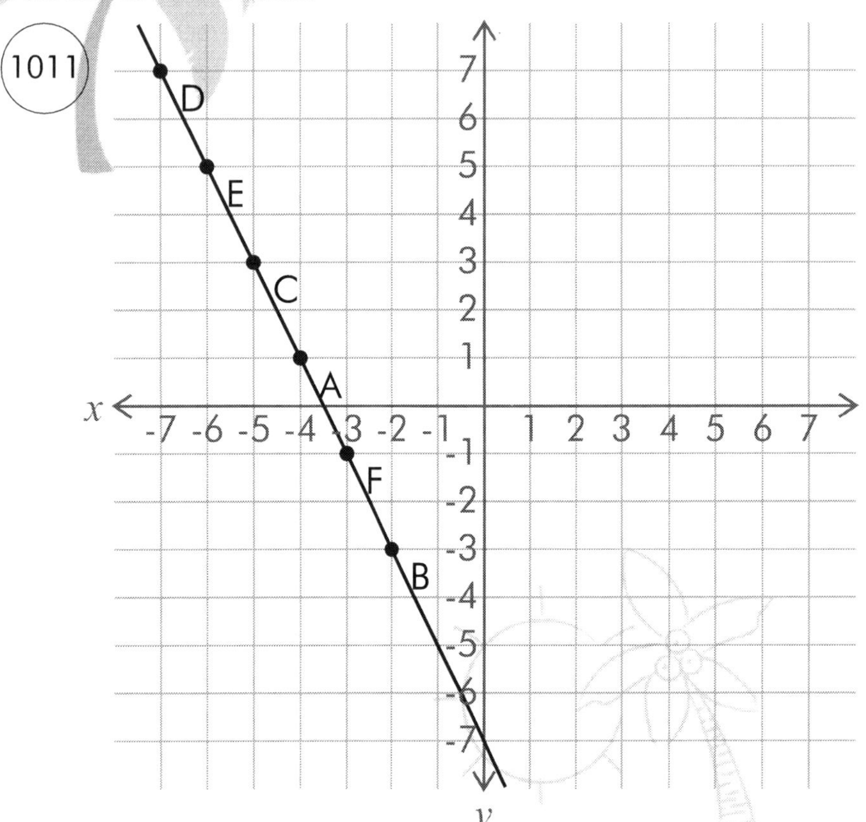

A = ______________ B = ______________

C = ______________ D = ______________

E = ______________ F = ______________

SUMMER
MATH SUCCESS

Name: ________________ Class: __________

Plot Lines

Plot and draw the lines.

1012

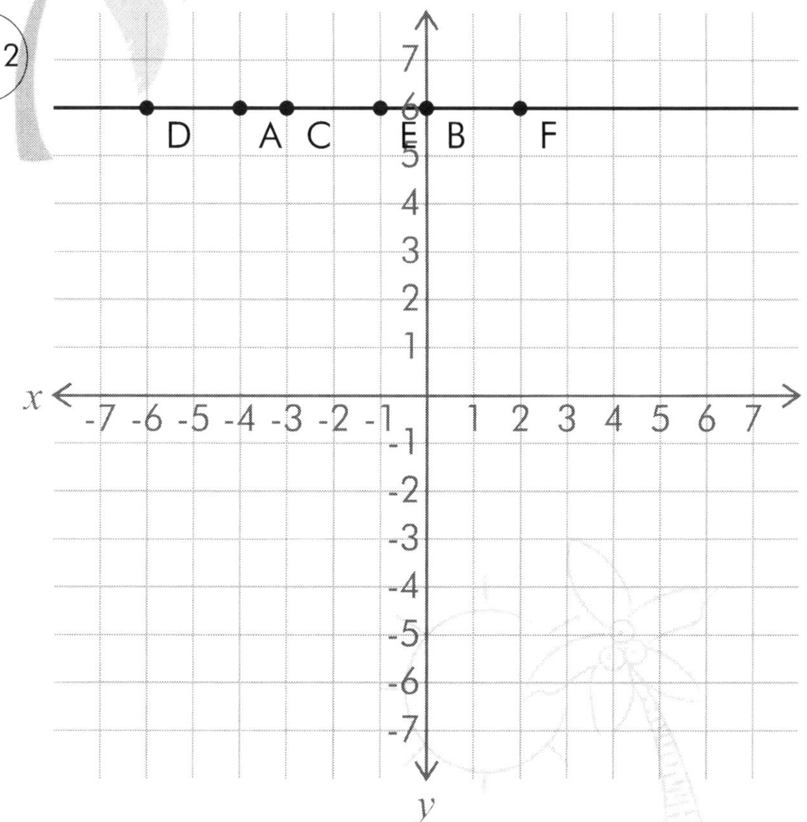

A = ____________ B = ____________

C = ____________ D = ____________

E = ____________ F = ____________

SUMMER MATH SUCCESS

Name: ____________ Class: ________

Plot Lines

Plot and draw the lines.

1013

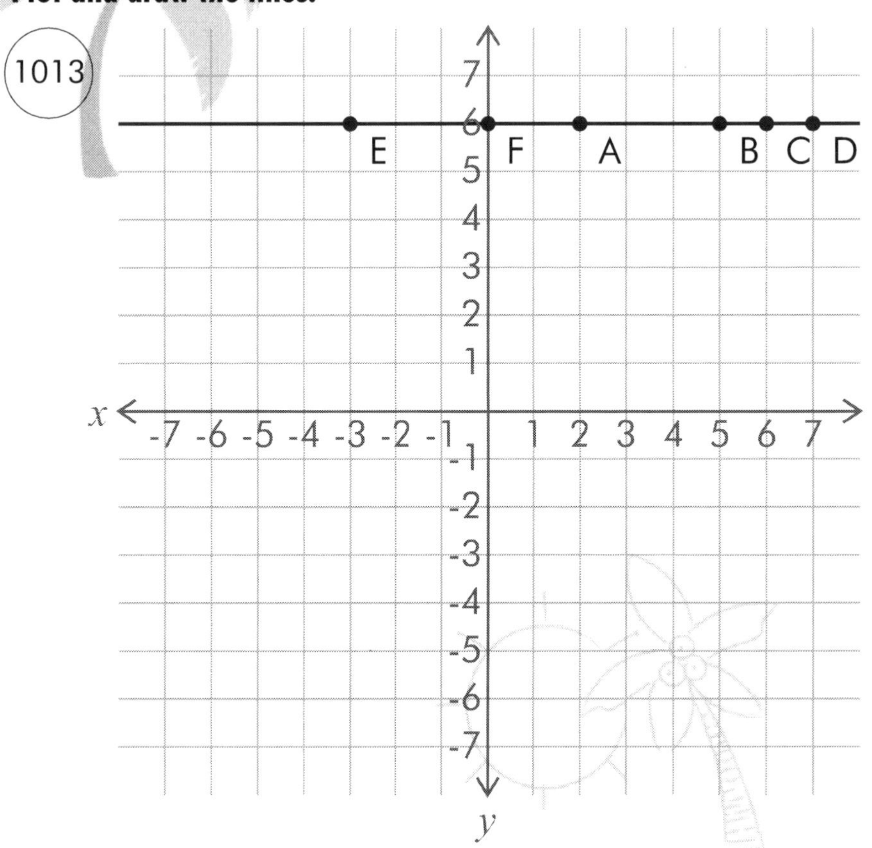

A = ____________ B = ____________

C = ____________ D = ____________

E = ____________ F = ____________

SUMMER MATH SUCCESS

Name: ____________ Class: ________

Exponents

Convert the values.

(1014) $6^2 =$ ____________

(1015) $37^3 =$ ____________

(1016) $9^2 =$ ____________

(1017) $21^2 =$ ____________

(1018) $20^3 =$ ____________

(1019) $57^2 =$ ____________

(1020) $32^3 =$ ____________

(1021) $7^2 =$ ____________

(1022) $35^2 =$ ____________

(1023) $23^2 =$ ____________

(1024) $71^2 =$ ____________

(1025) $75^3 =$ ____________

(1026) $11^3 =$ ____________

(1027) $83^3 =$ ____________

(1028) $16^3 =$ ____________

(1029) $28^3 =$ ____________

(1030) $37^2 =$ ____________

(1031) $68^2 =$ ____________

(1032) $40^2 =$ ____________

(1033) $13^3 =$ ____________

SUMMER MATH SUCCESS

Name: ____________ Class: ________

Exponents

Convert the values.

(1034) 4^2 = ____________

(1035) 58^3 = ____________

(1036) 25^2 = ____________

(1037) 68^3 = ____________

(1038) 38^3 = ____________

(1039) 66^2 = ____________

(1040) 23^2 = ____________

(1041) 52^2 = ____________

(1042) 71^2 = ____________

(1043) 33^3 = ____________

(1044) 34^2 = ____________

(1045) 65^3 = ____________

(1046) 19^3 = ____________

(1047) 1^2 = ____________

(1048) 55^3 = ____________

(1049) 59^3 = ____________

(1050) 35^2 = ____________

(1051) 39^3 = ____________

(1052) 61^2 = ____________

(1053) 50^3 = ____________

SUMMER MATH SUCCESS

Name: ________________ Class: __________

Exponents
Convert the values.

(1054) 8^2 = ____________________

(1055) 25^2 = ____________________

(1056) 29^2 = ____________________

(1057) 53^3 = ____________________

(1058) 62^3 = ____________________

(1059) 15^3 = ____________________

(1060) 73^3 = ____________________

(1061) 50^3 = ____________________

(1062) 14^3 = ____________________

(1063) 13^3 = ____________________

(1064) 99^3 = ____________________

(1065) 81^2 = ____________________

(1066) 45^2 = ____________________

(1067) 71^2 = ____________________

(1068) 22^2 = ____________________

(1069) 33^3 = ____________________

(1070) 59^3 = ____________________

(1071) 76^2 = ____________________

(1072) 86^2 = ____________________

(1073) 40^3 = ____________________

SUMMER MATH SUCCESS

Name: ____________ Class: ________

Exponents

Convert the values.

(1074) $65^2 =$ ____________

(1075) $66^2 =$ ____________

(1076) $58^3 =$ ____________

(1077) $28^3 =$ ____________

(1078) $74^2 =$ ____________

(1079) $45^2 =$ ____________

(1080) $8^3 =$ ____________

(1081) $13^2 =$ ____________

(1082) $12^2 =$ ____________

(1083) $27^2 =$ ____________

(1084) $36^2 =$ ____________

(1085) $84^2 =$ ____________

(1086) $88^2 =$ ____________

(1087) $18^2 =$ ____________

(1088) $84^3 =$ ____________

(1089) $7^2 =$ ____________

(1090) $1^2 =$ ____________

(1091) $23^2 =$ ____________

(1092) $68^2 =$ ____________

(1093) $4^2 =$ ____________

SUMMER
MATH SUCCESS

Name: ____________ Class: ________

Exponents
Convert the values.

1094 55^2 = ____________

1095 23^3 = ____________

1096 79^2 = ____________

1097 43^3 = ____________

1098 30^3 = ____________

1099 90^3 = ____________

1100 22^3 = ____________

1101 10^2 = ____________

1102 48^2 = ____________

1103 14^2 = ____________

1104 64^2 = ____________

1105 22^2 = ____________

1106 99^2 = ____________

1107 74^3 = ____________

1108 52^3 = ____________

1109 21^2 = ____________

1110 53^3 = ____________

1111 82^2 = ____________

1112 49^3 = ____________

1113 50^2 = ____________

SUMMER MATH SUCCESS

Name: ______________ Class: __________

Scientific Notation

Provide the scientific notation for each value.

(1114) 492,000 = ____________

(1115) 3,346,000 = ____________

(1116) 1,486,000 = ____________

(1117) 7,162,000 = ____________

(1118) 7,600,000 = ____________

(1119) 664,000 = ____________

(1120) 1,249,000 = ____________

(1121) 9,250,000 = ____________

(1122) 9,800,000 = ____________

(1123) 8,120,000 = ____________

(1124) 3,200,000 = ____________

(1125) 6,780,000 = ____________

(1126) 8,200,000 = ____________

(1127) 3,589,000 = ____________

(1128) 7,400,000 = ____________

(1129) 9,890,000 = ____________

(1130) 3,490,000 = ____________

(1131) 5,020,000 = ____________

(1132) 4,530,000 = ____________

(1133) 1,543,000 = ____________

SUMMER MATH SUCCESS

Name: ____________ Class: ________

Scientific Notation

Provide the scientific notation for each value.

1134 5,000,000 = __________

1135 7,088,000 = __________

1136 5,760,000 = __________

1137 8,674,000 = __________

1138 5,925,000 = __________

1139 120,000 = __________

1140 1,795,000 = __________

1141 56,000 = __________

1142 230,000 = __________

1143 5,400,000 = __________

1144 2,030,000 = __________

1145 1,520,000 = __________

1146 4,940,000 = __________

1147 2,520,000 = __________

1148 9,140,000 = __________

1149 649,000 = __________

1150 9,900,000 = __________

1151 4,385,000 = __________

1152 8,920,000 = __________

1153 1,860,000 = __________

SUMMER MATH SUCCESS

Name: ____________ Class: ________

Scientific Notation

Provide the scientific notation for each value.

(1154) 1,169,000 = ____________

(1155) 6,067,000 = ____________

(1156) 5,460,000 = ____________

(1157) 3,030,000 = ____________

(1158) 5,370,000 = ____________

(1159) 5,500,000 = ____________

(1160) 4,520,000 = ____________

(1161) 9,400,000 = ____________

(1162) 8,400,000 = ____________

(1163) 8,800,000 = ____________

(1164) 7,300,000 = ____________

(1165) 9,200,000 = ____________

(1166) 2,400,000 = ____________

(1167) 19,000 = ____________

(1168) 4,600,000 = ____________

(1169) 9,740,000 = ____________

(1170) 9,000,000 = ____________

(1171) 540,000 = ____________

(1172) 9,600,000 = ____________

(1173) 3,380,000 = ____________

SUMMER MATH SUCCESS

Name: ______________ Class: ________

Scientific Notation

Provide the scientific notation for each value.

1174 $8.4 \times 10^6 =$ ________

1175 $8.5 \times 10^6 =$ ________

1176 $3.62 \times 10^6 =$ ________

1177 $2.3 \times 10^6 =$ ________

1178 $8.437 \times 10^6 =$ ________

1179 $5.668 \times 10^6 =$ ________

1180 $6.343 \times 10^6 =$ ________

1181 $9.78 \times 10^6 =$ ________

1182 $4.27 \times 10^6 =$ ________

1183 $3.5 \times 10^6 =$ ________

1184 $1.3 \times 10^6 =$ ________

1185 $6.123 \times 10^6 =$ ________

1186 $1.5 \times 10^6 =$ ________

1187 $6.04 \times 10^6 =$ ________

1188 $9.93 \times 10^6 =$ ________

1189 $1.075 \times 10^6 =$ ________

1190 $8.8 \times 10^6 =$ ________

1191 $3.64 \times 10^6 =$ ________

1192 $2.4 \times 10^6 =$ ________

1193 $8.33 \times 10^6 =$ ________

SUMMER
MATH SUCCESS

Name: ____________ Class: ________

Scientific Notation

Provide the scientific notation for each value.

1194 $7.7 \times 10^{6} =$ ________

1195 $4.7 \times 10^{6} =$ ________

1196 $6.5 \times 10^{4} =$ ________

1197 $5.392 \times 10^{6} =$ ________

1198 $3.19 \times 10^{6} =$ ________

1199 $4.92 \times 10^{5} =$ ________

1200 $7.8 \times 10^{6} =$ ________

1201 $5.14 \times 10^{6} =$ ________

1202 $7.15 \times 10^{6} =$ ________

1203 $8.5 \times 10^{6} =$ ________

1204 $8.94 \times 10^{6} =$ ________

1205 $3.96 \times 10^{6} =$ ________

1206 $7.161 \times 10^{6} =$ ________

1207 $7.43 \times 10^{5} =$ ________

1208 $5.42 \times 10^{6} =$ ________

1209 $2.6 \times 10^{6} =$ ________

1210 $5.162 \times 10^{6} =$ ________

1211 $5.2 \times 10^{6} =$ ________

1212 $7.39 \times 10^{6} =$ ________

1213 $9.7 \times 10^{6} =$ ________

SUMMER MATH SUCCESS

Name: ____________ Class: ________

Scientific Notation

Provide the scientific notation for each value.

(1214) $7.4 \times 10^{6} =$ ________

(1215) $3.27 \times 10^{6} =$ ________

(1216) $3.14 \times 10^{6} =$ ________

(1217) $9.547 \times 10^{6} =$ ________

(1218) $5.695 \times 10^{6} =$ ________

(1219) $8.84 \times 10^{6} =$ ________

(1220) $3.893 \times 10^{6} =$ ________

(1221) $6 \times 10^{6} =$ ________

(1222) $6.759 \times 10^{6} =$ ________

(1223) $4.3 \times 10^{6} =$ ________

(1224) $8.726 \times 10^{6} =$ ________

(1225) $4.398 \times 10^{6} =$ ________

(1226) $2.725 \times 10^{6} =$ ________

(1227) $9.42 \times 10^{5} =$ ________

(1228) $5.11 \times 10^{6} =$ ________

(1229) $8.8 \times 10^{6} =$ ________

(1230) $8.92 \times 10^{6} =$ ________

(1231) $3.4 \times 10^{6} =$ ________

(1232) $2.56 \times 10^{6} =$ ________

(1233) $1.6 \times 10^{6} =$ ________

SUMMER MATH SUCCESS

Name: ____________ Class: ________

Expressions - Single Step

Solve for the variable.

1234 $6 + x = 8$ ____________

1235 $4 - x = -1$ ____________

1236 $2 - x = -3$ ____________

1237 $x - 7 = 1$ ____________

1238 $6 + x = 13$ ____________

1239 $7 + x = 14$ ____________

1240 $x + 9 = 13$ ____________

1241 $3 - x = -6$ ____________

1242 $9 - x = 5$ ____________

1243 $8 + x = 9$ ____________

1244 $x - 8 = 0$ ____________

1245 $8 - x = -1$ ____________

1246 $x - 4 = 0$ ____________

1247 $x - 7 = -5$ ____________

1248 $x + 2 = 5$ ____________

1249 $6 - x = 3$ ____________

1250 $4 + x = 8$ ____________

1251 $x + 4 = 9$ ____________

1252 $2 - x = -1$ ____________

1253 $x - 5 = 2$ ____________

SUMMER MATH SUCCESS

Name: ____________ Class: ________

Expressions - Single Step

Solve for the variable.

1254 $x - 2 = 4$ ____________

1255 $x - 9 = -6$ ____________

1256 $4 + x = 12$ ____________

1257 $x + 6 = 13$ ____________

1258 $x + 1 = 2$ ____________

1259 $x + 5 = 8$ ____________

1260 $9 + x = 16$ ____________

1261 $1 - x = -7$ ____________

1262 $7 + x = 15$ ____________

1263 $5 + x = 10$ ____________

1264 $x + 2 = 9$ ____________

1265 $6 + x = 10$ ____________

1266 $x - 7 = -6$ ____________

1267 $x - 3 = 2$ ____________

1268 $2 + x = 9$ ____________

1269 $4 + x = 9$ ____________

1270 $x + 5 = 14$ ____________

1271 $5 + x = 8$ ____________

1272 $2 - x = -3$ ____________

1273 $6 - x = 2$ ____________

SUMMER MATH SUCCESS

Name: ________________ Class: __________

Expressions - Single Step

Solve for the variable.

1274 $x + 9 = 10$ ____________

1275 $x - 5 = 4$ ____________

1276 $x - 1 = 7$ ____________

1277 $x - 6 = -4$ ____________

1278 $4 + x = 13$ ____________

1279 $6 - x = 2$ ____________

1280 $6 + x = 15$ ____________

1281 $x - 9 = -7$ ____________

1282 $x + 5 = 10$ ____________

1283 $8 - x = 3$ ____________

1284 $2 + x = 5$ ____________

1285 $x + 5 = 9$ ____________

1286 $x + 7 = 9$ ____________

1287 $x + 2 = 3$ ____________

1288 $x + 5 = 8$ ____________

1289 $7 - x = 0$ ____________

1290 $x - 1 = 4$ ____________

1291 $x + 6 = 11$ ____________

1292 $x + 3 = 4$ ____________

1293 $x + 3 = 9$ ____________

SUMMER
MATH SUCCESS

Name: ________________ Class: __________

Expressions - Single Step

Solve for the variable.

1294 $x - 8 = -2$ ________________

1295 $8 - x = 7$ ________________

1296 $x - 5 = 2$ ________________

1297 $x - 6 = -1$ ________________

1298 $x + 8 = 13$ ________________

1299 $x + 1 = 7$ ________________

1300 $6 - x = -1$ ________________

1301 $x + 2 = 3$ ________________

1302 $x + 9 = 16$ ________________

1303 $x + 1 = 8$ ________________

1304 $x - 8 = 0$ ________________

1305 $6 - x = 3$ ________________

1306 $x + 5 = 6$ ________________

1307 $8 + x = 12$ ________________

1308 $x + 6 = 13$ ________________

1309 $3 - x = 1$ ________________

1310 $8 - x = 2$ ________________

1311 $3 + x = 8$ ________________

1312 $x - 4 = 5$ ________________

1313 $x + 3 = 10$ ________________

SUMMER MATH SUCCESS

Name: ____________ Class: ________

Expressions - Single Step

Solve for the variable.

(1314) $7 - x = 0$ ____________

(1315) $4 - x = -1$ ____________

(1316) $x - 4 = 0$ ____________

(1317) $x - 7 = 2$ ____________

(1318) $x - 7 = -2$ ____________

(1319) $9 - x = 7$ ____________

(1320) $x - 3 = -2$ ____________

(1321) $x - 2 = -1$ ____________

(1322) $x + 7 = 16$ ____________

(1323) $x - 7 = -6$ ____________

(1324) $x + 9 = 15$ ____________

(1325) $x + 4 = 12$ ____________

(1326) $x + 2 = 3$ ____________

(1327) $x - 2 = 2$ ____________

(1328) $x + 1 = 6$ ____________

(1329) $x + 7 = 8$ ____________

(1330) $6 + x = 7$ ____________

(1331) $2 + x = 10$ ____________

(1332) $x + 6 = 7$ ____________

(1333) $x - 6 = -4$ ____________

SUMMER MATH SUCCESS

Name: ____________ Class: ________

Number Problems

Solve.

1334 ___ A number increased by 23 is 26. Find the number.

1335 ___ Twenty-three less than a number is 28. Find the number.

1336 ___ The sum of a number and 26 is 51. Find the number.

1337 ___ A number increased by seven is 29. Find the number.

1338 ___ Thirteen less than a number is 7. Find the number.

1339 ___ Thirteen less than a number is 4. Find the number.

1340 ___ Eight less than a number is 18. Find the number.

1341 ___ A number increased by 21 is 48. Find the number.

1342 ___ One-half of a number is 15. Find the number.

1343 ___ A number diminished by 13 is 7. Find the number.

SUMMER MATH SUCCESS

Name: ________________ Class: __________

Number Problems

Solve.

1344 ____ The sum of a number and eight is 22. Find the number.

1345 ____ The sum of a number and 19 is 38. Find the number.

1346 ____ Two-fourths of a number is 10. Find the number.

1347 ____ One-half of a number is 3. Find the number.

1348 ____ A number increased by 27 is 45. Find the number.

1349 ____ Two-fifths of a number is 6. Find the number.

1350 ____ A number diminished by 4 is 25. Find the number.

1351 ____ The sum of a number and two is 19. Find the number.

1352 ____ Nineteen more than a number is 40. What is the number?

1353 ____ Eight less than a number is 9. Find the number.

SUMMER MATH SUCCESS

Name: ______________ Class: __________

Number Problems

Solve.

1354 ___ The sum of a number and 28 is 42. Find the number.

1355 ___ Twenty-nine more than a number is 51. What is the number?

1356 ___ A number decreased by 10 is 9. Find the number.

1357 ___ A number increased by four is 19. Find the number.

1358 ___ Twenty-four more than a number is 38. What is the number?

1359 ___ One-half of a number is 5. Find the number.

1360 ___ One-half of a number is 3. Find the number.

1361 ___ A number diminished by 20 is 16. Find the number.

1362 ___ Twenty-two more than a number is 48. What is the number?

1363 ___ One-half of a number is 7. Find the number.

SUMMER MATH SUCCESS

Name: ____________ Class: ____________

Pre-Algebra Equations (One Step) Addition and Subtraction

Solve for the variable.

1364 $8x + 4 = 20$ ____________

1365 $3 + x = 9$ ____________

1366 $x + 1 = 8$ ____________

1367 $15 - 2x = 1$ ____________

1368 $12 - 1x = 5$ ____________

1369 $9 - x = 5$ ____________

1370 $1x + 5 = 8$ ____________

1371 $x + 7 = 9$ ____________

1372 $4 + x = 7$ ____________

1373 $4x + 4 = 28$ ____________

1374 $4 + 7x = 32$ ____________

1375 $7 - x = 0$ ____________

1376 $4x + 4 = 40$ ____________

1377 $6 + x = 14$ ____________

1378 $9 - x = 3$ ____________

1379 $1 + x = 9$ ____________

1380 $4x - 4 = 28$ ____________

1381 $2 + 4x = 10$ ____________

1382 $8 + x = 15$ ____________

1383 $8 + 9x = 62$ ____________

SUMMER MATH SUCCESS

Name: ________________ Class: __________

Pre-Algebra Equations (One Step) Addition and Subtraction
Solve for the variable.

(1384) $9 + 8x = 33$ ____________

(1385) $5 + 1x = 8$ ____________

(1386) $x - 2 = 6$ ____________

(1387) $9 + 6x = 33$ ____________

(1388) $1 + x = 10$ ____________

(1389) $8 - x = 2$ ____________

(1390) $5x + 4 = 29$ ____________

(1391) $8 + x = 9$ ____________

(1392) $x - 3 = 1$ ____________

(1393) $x - 4 = 4$ ____________

(1394) $5 + x = 9$ ____________

(1395) $2 + x = 11$ ____________

(1396) $46 - 8x = 6$ ____________

(1397) $9 + x = 14$ ____________

(1398) $x + 7 = 8$ ____________

(1399) $55 - 6x = 7$ ____________

(1400) $3 + x = 4$ ____________

(1401) $6 - x = 3$ ____________

(1402) $8x - 5 = 51$ ____________

(1403) $x - 3 = 6$ ____________

SUMMER MATH SUCCESS

Name: ________________ Class: __________

Pre-Algebra Equations (One Step) Addition and Subtraction

Solve for the variable.

(1404) $6x + 2 = 14$ ____________

(1405) $9x - 9 = 27$ ____________

(1406) $31 - 5x = 1$ ____________

(1407) $4 + x = 7$ ____________

(1408) $x - 6 = 2$ ____________

(1409) $7 + x = 12$ ____________

(1410) $x - 3 = 3$ ____________

(1411) $9 - x = 1$ ____________

(1412) $6x + 4 = 46$ ____________

(1413) $x + 8 = 13$ ____________

(1414) $x - 4 = 5$ ____________

(1415) $6 - x = 4$ ____________

(1416) $9x + 8 = 17$ ____________

(1417) $7 - x = 0$ ____________

(1418) $x + 4 = 5$ ____________

(1419) $42 - 6x = 0$ ____________

(1420) $9 - x = 3$ ____________

(1421) $x - 2 = 7$ ____________

(1422) $8 - x = 7$ ____________

(1423) $x + 4 = 9$ ____________

SUMMER
MATH SUCCESS

Name: ____________ Class: ________

Pre-Algebra Equations (One Step) Addition and Subtraction
Solve for the variable.

1424 $2 + x = 3$ ____________

1425 $7x + 6 = 55$ ____________

1426 $x - 4 = 4$ ____________

1427 $x - 5 = 0$ ____________

1428 $x - 3 = 2$ ____________

1429 $7x - 4 = 59$ ____________

1430 $4 + x = 9$ ____________

1431 $x + 2 = 6$ ____________

1432 $x + 5 = 9$ ____________

1433 $x + 1 = 3$ ____________

1434 $3 + x = 10$ ____________

1435 $x + 7 = 16$ ____________

1436 $4 + x = 11$ ____________

1437 $5 + x = 11$ ____________

1438 $8 + x = 15$ ____________

1439 $1 + x = 10$ ____________

1440 $23 - 5x = 3$ ____________

1441 $6x + 1 = 7$ ____________

1442 $7 - 1x = 2$ ____________

1443 $x + 6 = 14$ ____________

SUMMER MATH SUCCESS

Name: ____________ Class: ________

Pre-Algebra Equations (One Step) Addition and Subtraction
Solve for the variable.

1444 $5 - x = 1$ ____________

1445 $4x + 9 = 17$ ____________

1446 $4x + 6 = 18$ ____________

1447 $9x - 7 = 65$ ____________

1448 $53 - 7x = 4$ ____________

1449 $9x - 1 = 35$ ____________

1450 $9 + x = 17$ ____________

1451 $6x + 8 = 50$ ____________

1452 $4 - x = 3$ ____________

1453 $3 - x = 2$ ____________

1454 $9 - x = 3$ ____________

1455 $4 + x = 8$ ____________

1456 $x + 4 = 6$ ____________

1457 $9 - x = 8$ ____________

1458 $9 - x = 2$ ____________

1459 $5 + x = 14$ ____________

1460 $9 + x = 10$ ____________

1461 $4x + 7 = 27$ ____________

1462 $x - 5 = 4$ ____________

1463 $x + 7 = 14$ ____________

SUMMER MATH SUCCESS

Name: ______________ Class: __________

Pre-Algebra Equations (One Step) Addition and Subtraction

Solve for the variable.

(1464) $9 - x = 5$ ______________

(1465) $17 - 3x = 5$ ______________

(1466) $15 - 3x = 9$ ______________

(1467) $7x + 5 = 47$ ______________

(1468) $x + 4 = 5$ ______________

(1469) $9 + 4x = 33$ ______________

(1470) $2x - 5 = 5$ ______________

(1471) $x - 7 = 2$ ______________

(1472) $1x + 9 = 11$ ______________

(1473) $x + 9 = 17$ ______________

(1474) $4 + 9x = 49$ ______________

(1475) $x - 8 = 0$ ______________

(1476) $11 - 1x = 7$ ______________

(1477) $1 + 3x = 16$ ______________

(1478) $2 + x = 7$ ______________

(1479) $9x - 3 = 6$ ______________

(1480) $9x + 6 = 51$ ______________

(1481) $4x - 2 = 34$ ______________

(1482) $8 + x = 17$ ______________

(1483) $1x + 2 = 9$ ______________

SUMMER MATH SUCCESS

Name: ________________ Class: __________

Pre-Algebra Equations (One Step) Addition and Subtraction

Solve for the variable.

1484 $1x - 6 = 0$ ____________

1485 $1 + 8x = 57$ ____________

1486 $8 - x = 1$ ____________

1487 $8 - x = 2$ ____________

1488 $8x - 9 = 7$ ____________

1489 $2x + 4 = 6$ ____________

1490 $x + 3 = 10$ ____________

1491 $5 + 1x = 8$ ____________

1492 $8x - 1 = 39$ ____________

1493 $2x - 1 = 17$ ____________

1494 $5 + 1x = 12$ ____________

1495 $8 + 2x = 16$ ____________

1496 $15 - 9x = 6$ ____________

1497 $3x + 8 = 23$ ____________

1498 $x + 9 = 11$ ____________

1499 $3 + x = 11$ ____________

1500 $6 + 8x = 38$ ____________

1501 $x - 2 = 5$ ____________

1502 $14 - 4x = 2$ ____________

1503 $9 + x = 16$ ____________

SUMMER MATH SUCCESS

Name: ____________ Class: ________

Pre-Algebra Equations (One Step) Addition and Subtraction

Solve for the variable.

1504 $x + 7 = 16$ ____________

1505 $3x - 7 = 8$ ____________

1506 $8 - x = 2$ ____________

1507 $x + 7 = 10$ ____________

1508 $9 + 3x = 24$ ____________

1509 $6 + 3x = 27$ ____________

1510 $x + 5 = 10$ ____________

1511 $4x + 7 = 39$ ____________

1512 $9x - 5 = 49$ ____________

1513 $x + 4 = 12$ ____________

1514 $21 - 2x = 7$ ____________

1515 $4 - x = 1$ ____________

1516 $2 + x = 11$ ____________

1517 $1 + x = 10$ ____________

1518 $4 + x = 13$ ____________

1519 $7 + x = 9$ ____________

1520 $4 + 2x = 16$ ____________

1521 $7 - x = 4$ ____________

1522 $3 + 4x = 11$ ____________

1523 $12 - 5x = 7$ ____________

SUMMER MATH SUCCESS

Name: ________________ Class: __________

Pre-Algebra Equations (One Step) Addition and Subtraction

Solve for the variable.

(1524) $3 + x = 8$ ____________

(1525) $5x + 9 = 44$ ____________

(1526) $9x + 2 = 83$ ____________

(1527) $5 + 5x = 20$ ____________

(1528) $2 + 2x = 18$ ____________

(1529) $x - 5 = 2$ ____________

(1530) $x - 4 = 3$ ____________

(1531) $x + 6 = 12$ ____________

(1532) $3x + 9 = 33$ ____________

(1533) $2 + x = 3$ ____________

(1534) $9 - x = 7$ ____________

(1535) $1 + 6x = 37$ ____________

(1536) $2x - 8 = 6$ ____________

(1537) $5 + 6x = 41$ ____________

(1538) $x - 1 = 6$ ____________

(1539) $9x - 1 = 62$ ____________

(1540) $14 - 1x = 9$ ____________

(1541) $x + 5 = 7$ ____________

(1542) $66 - 8x = 2$ ____________

(1543) $x - 7 = 2$ ____________

SUMMER
MATH SUCCESS

Name: ________________ Class: __________

Pre-Algebra Equations (One Step) Addition and Subtraction

Solve for the variable.

1544 $9x + 7 = 88$ ____________

1545 $3 - x = 2$ ____________

1546 $22 - 2x = 6$ ____________

1547 $8 - x = 2$ ____________

1548 $9 - x = 8$ ____________

1549 $9 - x = 5$ ____________

1550 $5 + 1x = 9$ ____________

1551 $7x + 3 = 45$ ____________

1552 $2 + 8x = 50$ ____________

1553 $3 + x = 8$ ____________

1554 $31 - 6x = 1$ ____________

1555 $6 + x = 8$ ____________

1556 $2 - x = 1$ ____________

1557 $3x + 8 = 32$ ____________

1558 $x - 8 = 1$ ____________

1559 $7 + x = 13$ ____________

1560 $x + 8 = 10$ ____________

1561 $5x + 1 = 41$ ____________

1562 $9 + 4x = 33$ ____________

1563 $8 + x = 17$ ____________

SUMMER MATH SUCCESS

Name: ____________ Class: ________

Pre-Algebra Equations (One Step) Multiplication and Division
Solve for the variable.

1564 $x \times 4 = 28$ ____________

1565 $63 \div x = 7$ ____________

1566 $x \div 5 = 2$ ____________

1567 $28 \div x = 7$ ____________

1568 $2 \times x = 8$ ____________

1569 $7 \times x = 35$ ____________

1570 $54 \div x = 6$ ____________

1571 $2x + 6 = 20$ ____________

1572 $17 - 4x = 5$ ____________

1573 $1 \times x = 2$ ____________

1574 $1 \div x = 1$ ____________

1575 $48 \div x = 8$ ____________

1576 $3 + 6x = 51$ ____________

1577 $6x - 6 = 30$ ____________

1578 $5x + 1 = 31$ ____________

1579 $2 + 5x = 27$ ____________

1580 $33 - 6x = 3$ ____________

1581 $4x - 9 = 23$ ____________

1582 $1x + 7 = 8$ ____________

1583 $2 + 8x = 58$ ____________

SUMMER
MATH SUCCESS

Name: ________________ Class: __________

Pre-Algebra Equations (One Step) Multiplication and Division
Solve for the variable.

(1584) $x \times 9 = 18$ ____________

(1585) $3x + 4 = 10$ ____________

(1586) $5x + 5 = 10$ ____________

(1587) $8 \times x = 32$ ____________

(1588) $63 - 8x = 7$ ____________

(1589) $5 \div x = 1$ ____________

(1590) $x \times 6 = 6$ ____________

(1591) $x \times 8 = 40$ ____________

(1592) $4x + 7 = 35$ ____________

(1593) $48 - 6x = 0$ ____________

(1594) $1 + 6x = 55$ ____________

(1595) $39 - 4x = 7$ ____________

(1596) $x \times 8 = 24$ ____________

(1597) $x \times 3 = 24$ ____________

(1598) $x \div 2 = 2$ ____________

(1599) $x \times 3 = 9$ ____________

(1600) $3 + 2x = 21$ ____________

(1601) $4 + 2x = 18$ ____________

(1602) $5x - 2 = 3$ ____________

(1603) $12 \div x = 2$ ____________

SUMMER MATH SUCCESS

Name: ______________ Class: __________

Pre-Algebra Equations (One Step) Multiplication and Division

Solve for the variable.

1604 $x \div 1 = 3$ ______________

1605 $6 + 9x = 60$ ______________

1606 $x \div 7 = 4$ ______________

1607 $x \div 3 = 2$ ______________

1608 $5 \times x = 15$ ______________

1609 $x \div 8 = 2$ ______________

1610 $5 \times x = 25$ ______________

1611 $4x - 1 = 23$ ______________

1612 $1 \times x = 2$ ______________

1613 $6 - 2x = 0$ ______________

1614 $4 \times x = 8$ ______________

1615 $62 - 7x = 6$ ______________

1616 $9 + 6x = 45$ ______________

1617 $x \times 8 = 24$ ______________

1618 $2x - 2 = 4$ ______________

1619 $x \div 7 = 9$ ______________

1620 $1 \div x = 1$ ______________

1621 $3x + 7 = 10$ ______________

1622 $32 - 4x = 8$ ______________

1623 $36 \div x = 4$ ______________

SUMMER MATH SUCCESS

Name: ____________ Class: ________

Pre-Algebra Equations (One Step) Multiplication and Division
Solve for the variable.

(1624) $33 - 6x = 9$ ________

(1625) $8x + 7 = 47$ ________

(1626) $9 + 6x = 63$ ________

(1627) $5x - 1 = 44$ ________

(1628) $14 \div x = 7$ ________

(1629) $x \times 6 = 36$ ________

(1630) $14 - 7x = 7$ ________

(1631) $19 - 4x = 7$ ________

(1632) $x \div 1 = 1$ ________

(1633) $x \div 4 = 6$ ________

(1634) $48 \div x = 6$ ________

(1635) $8 \div x = 1$ ________

(1636) $3x + 5 = 20$ ________

(1637) $5 + 3x = 23$ ________

(1638) $6x + 8 = 14$ ________

(1639) $7x + 6 = 41$ ________

(1640) $6 \div x = 2$ ________

(1641) $x \div 2 = 6$ ________

(1642) $9x + 7 = 70$ ________

(1643) $7 + 1x = 11$ ________

SUMMER MATH SUCCESS

Name: ______________ Class: __________

Pre-Algebra Equations (One Step) Multiplication and Division
Solve for the variable.

1644 $7 \times x = 14$ ______________

1645 $9x - 7 = 38$ ______________

1646 $9x + 7 = 70$ ______________

1647 $9 \times x = 18$ ______________

1648 $8 - 2x = 6$ ______________

1649 $x \div 5 = 1$ ______________

1650 $5x - 2 = 13$ ______________

1651 $5x + 1 = 21$ ______________

1652 $3 \times x = 18$ ______________

1653 $3 + 9x = 75$ ______________

1654 $2 \times x = 2$ ______________

1655 $6x + 5 = 59$ ______________

1656 $x \div 5 = 8$ ______________

1657 $6x + 3 = 45$ ______________

1658 $3 \times x = 15$ ______________

1659 $4 \times x = 36$ ______________

1660 $x \div 2 = 8$ ______________

1661 $x \div 6 = 4$ ______________

1662 $4x + 2 = 22$ ______________

1663 $4 + 3x = 28$ ______________

SUMMER
MATH SUCCESS

Name: ____________ Class: ________

Pre-Algebra Equations (One Step) Multiplication and Division
Solve for the variable.

(1664) $5x + 2 = 42$ ____________ (1665) $x \div 5 = 1$ ____________

(1666) $5 + 1x = 8$ ____________ (1667) $6 \div x = 2$ ____________

(1668) $6 \times x = 24$ ____________ (1669) $x \div 6 = 9$ ____________

(1670) $x \times 6 = 36$ ____________ (1671) $3x + 7 = 28$ ____________

(1672) $18 \div x = 3$ ____________ (1673) $18 - 2x = 8$ ____________

(1674) $x \div 8 = 3$ ____________ (1675) $7x + 3 = 24$ ____________

(1676) $x \div 1 = 5$ ____________ (1677) $x \div 4 = 5$ ____________

(1678) $6 \times x = 12$ ____________ (1679) $19 - 8x = 3$ ____________

(1680) $9x - 1 = 8$ ____________ (1681) $5x + 5 = 25$ ____________

(1682) $x \times 8 = 72$ ____________ (1683) $14 \div x = 7$ ____________

SUMMER MATH SUCCESS

Name: ____________ Class: ________

Pre-Algebra Equations (One Step) Multiplication and Division

Solve for the variable.

1684) $x \times 2 = 14$ ____________

1685) $4 \div x = 1$ ____________

1686) $15 - 1x = 8$ ____________

1687) $4 - 1x = 2$ ____________

1688) $3x - 1 = 23$ ____________

1689) $67 - 9x = 4$ ____________

1690) $68 - 9x = 5$ ____________

1691) $2x + 3 = 21$ ____________

1692) $12 - 6x = 0$ ____________

1693) $6x - 3 = 9$ ____________

1694) $x \div 6 = 1$ ____________

1695) $8 \times x = 32$ ____________

1696) $4 \times x = 20$ ____________

1697) $5 \times x = 10$ ____________

1698) $x \div 6 = 3$ ____________

1699) $53 - 7x = 4$ ____________

1700) $x \div 9 = 8$ ____________

1701) $4 \times x = 36$ ____________

1702) $8 - 2x = 2$ ____________

1703) $5 + 2x = 17$ ____________

SUMMER MATH SUCCESS

Name: ____________ Class: ________

Pre-Algebra Equations (One Step) Multiplication and Division

Solve for the variable.

1704 $9 + 8x = 49$ ____________

1705 $4 \times x = 32$ ____________

1706 $x \div 6 = 9$ ____________

1707 $81 - 8x = 9$ ____________

1708 $3 \times x = 18$ ____________

1709 $9x + 9 = 45$ ____________

1710 $8 \div x = 2$ ____________

1711 $7x + 8 = 43$ ____________

1712 $x \div 5 = 6$ ____________

1713 $7 + 5x = 12$ ____________

1714 $72 \div x = 8$ ____________

1715 $3 \times x = 6$ ____________

1716 $5 + 3x = 11$ ____________

1717 $6 + 3x = 30$ ____________

1718 $x \div 6 = 4$ ____________

1719 $21 \div x = 3$ ____________

1720 $x \times 1 = 2$ ____________

1721 $x \div 1 = 3$ ____________

1722 $8x - 1 = 39$ ____________

1723 $x \div 7 = 7$ ____________

SUMMER MATH SUCCESS

Name: ____________ Class: ________

Pre-Algebra Equations (One Step) Multiplication and Division

Solve for the variable.

1724 $x \times 6 = 12$ ____________

1725 $4x + 8 = 36$ ____________

1726 $x \div 9 = 3$ ____________

1727 $43 - 8x = 3$ ____________

1728 $12 \div x = 3$ ____________

1729 $1 + 4x = 25$ ____________

1730 $6 + 3x = 18$ ____________

1731 $15 - 3x = 6$ ____________

1732 $2 + 1x = 10$ ____________

1733 $x \div 8 = 9$ ____________

1734 $18 \div x = 9$ ____________

1735 $1x + 3 = 11$ ____________

1736 $x \div 4 = 1$ ____________

1737 $5 \times x = 45$ ____________

1738 $56 \div x = 7$ ____________

1739 $x \times 5 = 25$ ____________

1740 $6x + 1 = 43$ ____________

1741 $2x + 5 = 19$ ____________

1742 $2 \times x = 10$ ____________

1743 $26 - 3x = 2$ ____________

SUMMER MATH SUCCESS

Name: ____________ Class: ________

Pre-Algebra Equations (One Step) Multiplication and Division
Solve for the variable.

1744 $2 + 7x = 37$ ____________

1745 $3x + 9 = 33$ ____________

1746 $8 \div x = 2$ ____________

1747 $3x - 6 = 0$ ____________

1748 $x \times 9 = 18$ ____________

1749 $x \div 6 = 4$ ____________

1750 $4 \times x = 12$ ____________

1751 $x \times 8 = 24$ ____________

1752 $x \times 3 = 21$ ____________

1753 $4x - 3 = 33$ ____________

1754 $x \times 5 = 45$ ____________

1755 $x \div 6 = 5$ ____________

1756 $x \div 7 = 2$ ____________

1757 $7 \times x = 28$ ____________

1758 $3x - 5 = 4$ ____________

1759 $6x - 1 = 11$ ____________

1760 $13 - 2x = 7$ ____________

1761 $3 + 7x = 59$ ____________

1762 $5x + 9 = 14$ ____________

1763 $3x - 7 = 17$ ____________

SUMMER MATH SUCCESS

Name: ______________ Class: __________

Pre-Algebra Equations (One Step) Multiplication and Division

Solve for the variable.

1764 $6 + 8x = 38$ __________

1765 $x \times 3 = 15$ __________

1766 $x \div 7 = 6$ __________

1767 $9 \times x = 18$ __________

1768 $x \div 6 = 1$ __________

1769 $37 - 8x = 5$ __________

1770 $5 \times x = 5$ __________

1771 $3x + 4 = 7$ __________

1772 $9 \times x = 36$ __________

1773 $x \times 3 = 6$ __________

1774 $4 \times x = 12$ __________

1775 $8x - 9 = 31$ __________

1776 $1x + 4 = 10$ __________

1777 $20 \div x = 5$ __________

1778 $x \div 8 = 4$ __________

1779 $4 + 2x = 18$ __________

1780 $x \times 7 = 14$ __________

1781 $x \div 8 = 6$ __________

1782 $1x + 6 = 11$ __________

1783 $x \div 6 = 7$ __________

SUMMER MATH SUCCESS

Name: ____________ Class: ________

Pre-Algebra Equations (One Step) Multiplication and Division

Solve for the variable.

(1784) $65 - 8x = 9$ ________

(1785) $29 - 6x = 5$ ________

(1786) $24 \div x = 4$ ________

(1787) $49 \div x = 7$ ________

(1788) $6 + 9x = 51$ ________

(1789) $1x - 2 = 5$ ________

(1790) $x \times 6 = 24$ ________

(1791) $4 + 5x = 44$ ________

(1792) $8 + 7x = 22$ ________

(1793) $42 \div x = 6$ ________

(1794) $14 - 2x = 8$ ________

(1795) $2 + 4x = 34$ ________

(1796) $71 - 7x = 8$ ________

(1797) $10 \div x = 5$ ________

(1798) $8x - 3 = 61$ ________

(1799) $7 \times x = 56$ ________

(1800) $x \times 3 = 12$ ________

(1801) $35 - 7x = 0$ ________

(1802) $3 \times x = 6$ ________

(1803) $6 \times x = 18$ ________

SUMMER
MATH SUCCESS

Name: ____________ Class: ____________

Pre-Algebra Equations (One Step) Multiplication and Division
Solve for the variable.

1804 $4 + 1x = 5$ ____________

1805 $2 \times x = 12$ ____________

1806 $x \times 2 = 4$ ____________

1807 $30 \div x = 6$ ____________

1808 $5 + 7x = 12$ ____________

1809 $3x + 2 = 29$ ____________

1810 $6x + 7 = 37$ ____________

1811 $5 \times x = 20$ ____________

1812 $7 \times x = 63$ ____________

1813 $x \times 6 = 36$ ____________

1814 $3 \times x = 6$ ____________

1815 $x \div 9 = 9$ ____________

1816 $4 + 5x = 44$ ____________

1817 $8 \times x = 32$ ____________

1818 $8x + 9 = 25$ ____________

1819 $5x + 6 = 46$ ____________

1820 $2x + 8 = 22$ ____________

1821 $17 - 4x = 1$ ____________

1822 $9x - 5 = 67$ ____________

1823 $5x - 4 = 11$ ____________

SUMMER MATH SUCCESS

Name: ____________ Class: ________

Pre-Algebra Equations (Two Sides)

Solve for the variable.

1824 $5 + 9x = 125 - 6x$

1825 $44 + x = 6x + 9$

1826 $2 + 3x + 4 = 24 + x$

1827 $42 - x = 3x + 6$

1828 $2 + 8x = 3x + 42$

1829 $16 + x = 5x$

1830 $7 + 2x + 8 = 16 - x + 11$

1831 $15 + 3x = 4x + 7$

1832 $2 + 6x = 2x + 14$

1833 $5x + 10 = 6 + 7x$

SUMMER MATH SUCCESS

Name: ______________ Class: ________

Pre-Algebra Equations (Two Sides)

Solve for the variable.

1834 $65 - 3x = 2 + 4x$

1835 $36 + 2x = 6 + 8x$

1836 $5 + 7x = 35 + x$

1837 $6 + 6x + 2 = 53 + x$

1838 $4 + 2x = 28 - x$

1839 $24 + x = 5x$

1840 $49 + x = 8x$

1841 $9 + 9x = 21 + 5x$

1842 $5x = 12 - x$

1843 $13 + 8x = 9x + 6$

SUMMER MATH SUCCESS

Name: ____________ Class: ________

Pre-Algebra Equations (Two Sides)

Solve for the variable.

1844 $29 + 6x = 5 + 9x$

1845 $7x + 4 = 28 - x$

1846 $17 + x + 5 = 8 + 5x + 2$

1847 $17 - x + 12 = 9 + 2x + 8$

1848 $58 - x + 17 = 8 + 6x + 4$

1849 $4 + x = 2x$

1850 $14 - x = 2x + 8$

1851 $28 + x = 8x$

1852 $2 + 3x = 22 - x$

1853 $8x = 42 + x$

SUMMER MATH SUCCESS

Name: ____________________ Class: __________

Pre-Algebra Equations (Two Sides)

Solve for the variable.

1854 $4x + 4 = 13 + x$

1855 $39 + x = 9 + 4x + 6$

1856 $8 + x = 5x$

1857 $9x + 6 = 7x + 16$

1858 $3x + 25 = 9x + 7$

1859 $8x = 54 - x$

1860 $3 + 2x + 9 = 30 - x$

1861 $6x = 40 + x$

1862 $28 - x = 8 + 2x + 5$

1863 $7 + x = 2x$

SUMMER MATH SUCCESS

Name: ____________ Class: ________

Pre-Algebra Equations (Two Sides)

Solve for the variable.

1864 $6 + 8x = 27 + x$

1865 $65 - x = 6 + 8x + 5$

1866 $30 - x = 7 + 4x + 8$

1867 $3 + 7x = 43 - x$

1868 $8x = 28 + x$

1869 $67 + x + -4 = 4 + 7x + 5$

1870 $7x = 42 + x$

1871 $4x + 7 = 42 - x$

1872 $3x = 14 + x$

1873 $67 - x = 8x + 4$

SUMMER
MATH SUCCESS

Name: ____________ Class: ________

Pre-Algebra Equations (Two Sides)
Solve for the variable.

1874 $20 + x = 6x$

1875 $9x + 4 = 157 - 8x$

1876 $6x + 9 = 16 + 5x$

1877 $67 - 6x = 2 + 7x$

1878 $7x = 24 + x$

1879 $7x = 16 - x$

1880 $2 + 4x + 8 = 36 - x + 9$

1881 $8x = 36 - x$

1882 $3x + 28 = 8x + 3$

1883 $7 + 3x + 6 = 31 + x$

SUMMER MATH SUCCESS

Name: ____________ Class: ________

Pre-Algebra Equations (Two Sides)

Solve for the variable.

1884 $7x + 10 = 7 + 8x$

1885 $23 + x = 3x + 7$

1886 $3x + 7 = 35 - x$

1887 $46 + x = 9 + 6x + 2$

1888 $37 - 2x = 7 + 4x$

1889 $9 + 3x + 3 = 32 - x$

1890 $5x + 9 = 17 + x$

1891 $23 + x = 4 + 3x + 5$

1892 $11 - x = 3x + 3$

1893 $29 - 3x = 4x + 8$

SUMMER
MATH SUCCESS

Name: ____________ Class: ________

Pre-Algebra Equations (Two Sides)

Solve for the variable.

1894 $5x = 12 + x$

1895 $59 - 2x = 9 + 8x$

1896 $7x + 2 = 28 - 6x$

1897 $6 + 2x = 11 + x$

1898 $58 + x = 5 + 8x + 4$

1899 $28 - x = 7 + 2x$

1900 $8x = 63 + x$

1901 $8 + 2x = 20 - x$

1902 $3x = 14 + x$

1903 $45 + x = 7 + 5x + 2$

SUMMER MATH SUCCESS

Name: ________________ Class: __________

Pre-Algebra Equations (Two Sides)

Solve for the variable.

1904 $9x + 5 = 20 + 6x$

1905 $3x = 16 - x$

1906 $41 + x = 6 + 5x + 7$

1907 $6x = 28 - x$

1908 $6x + 8 = 64 - x$

1909 $18 + x = 4x$

1910 $54 - x = 5x$

1911 $4 + 6x + 9 = 34 - x + 14$

1912 $3x = 24 - x$

1913 $74 - 8x = 9x + 6$

SUMMER MATH SUCCESS

Name: ________________ Class: ________

Pre-Algebra Equations (Two Sides)

Solve for the variable.

1914) $4 + 8x + 8 = 30 - x$

1915) $4 + 2x + 4 = 8 - x + 6$

1916) $46 + x + 3 = 4 + 7x + 9$

1917) $9 + 8x = 129 - 7x$

1918) $3x + 11 = 3 + 7x$

1919) $9x + 7 = 14 + 8x$

1920) $51 + x = 2 + 8x$

1921) $6x = 35 + x$

1922) $16 - x + 12 = 6 + 2x + 7$

1923) $3x = 18 + x$

SUMMER MATH SUCCESS

Name: ____________ Class: ________

Simplifying Expressions

1924 $x + 2 + x$

1925 $-6 + 8x - 6x - 9 - 6x$

1926 $-7 - 6x + 2x - 1 + 4x$

1927 $8x - 7x$

1928 $3 - 4(4x - 4)$

1929 $4 + 6x - 7x + 3 - 9x$

1930 $7x + 4 + 6x + 9 + 9x + 3$

SUMMER
MATH SUCCESS

Name: ______________ Class: __________

Simplifying Expressions

(1931) $8x - 6 - 3x + 3 - 3$

(1932) $2 + 7x - 8x + 7 - 3x$

(1933) $1 + 8x - 3x + 8 - 2x$

(1934) $x - 8x$

(1935) $6 + 6(-2x + 8)$

(1936) $3 + 7x - 9 + 8x - 7 + 5x$

(1937) $2x - 4 + 7x - 4 + 7x + 7$

SUMMER MATH SUCCESS

Name: ____________________ Class: __________

Simplifying Expressions

1938 $x - 8 - 5x + 4 - 5$

1939 $1 - 5x + 1 - x + 9 - 8x$

1940 $-8 + 9x + 5 - 5x$

1941 $5 + 4x - 4 + 4x - 3 + 7x$

1942 $5 - 3(6x - 4)$

1943 $1 + 8x - 7 + x - 6 + 5x$

1944 $3x + 2 - 7 - 6x + 4x$

SUMMER MATH SUCCESS

Name: ____________________ Class: ___________

Simplifying Expressions

1945 $6 + 7(9x + 5)$

1946 $6 + 5x - 3 + x$

1947 $-x - 3 - 8 - 3x$

1948 $5 + x - 7 + 5x$

1949 $-1 + 2x - 3x - 9 + 5x$

1950 $-8 - 4x + 7x - 3 + 5x$

1951 $2 + 5(7x + 5)$

SUMMER
MATH SUCCESS

Name: ____________ Class: ________

Simplifying Expressions

1952 $2 + 7x - 6 + 7x$

1953 $5x - 1 - 7x + 6$

1954 $2 + 1(-2x + 6)$

1955 $8x - 6 - 9x + 7$

1956 $6x - 5 - 5x + 2$

1957 $9x - 8 - 4x + 6 - 3$

1958 $8 + 7x - 2 + 7x - 9 + 9x$

SUMMER MATH SUCCESS

Name: ____________ Class: ________

Simplifying Expressions

1959 $6x + 3 + 7x + 3 + 7x + 4$

1960 $-8x + x$

1961 $6x + x$

1962 $2x + 3 - 4x - 4 + 7x - 9$

1963 $9x - 6 - 5x + 8 - 8$

1964 $3 + 8x - 4x + 8 - 2x$

1965 $-1 + 7 - 9x + 3x - 8 + 6x$

SUMMER MATH SUCCESS

Name: ______________ Class: __________

Simplifying Expressions

1966 $x - 8x$

1967 $x + 3x$

1968 $2x + 4 + x$

1969 $5x - 2x + 1 + 1$

1970 $3 + 5x + 3 + 9x$

1971 $x - 7x + 2x - 5 + 6$

1972 $-8x + 3 - 4x$

SUMMER
MATH SUCCESS

Name: ____________ Class: ________

Simplifying Expressions

1973 $x + 1 + 2x$

1974 $-4 + 1 - 8x + x - 8 + 3x$

1975 $5 + 9x - x + 4 - 2x$

1976 $4x - x$

1977 $-8x + x$

1978 $x - 2x + 8x + 2 + 1$

1979 $-9x - 3x$

SUMMER
MATH SUCCESS

Name: ________________ Class: __________

Simplifying Expressions

1980 $-5x - 4 - 1 - x$

1981 $7x - 7 - 3x + 3$

1982 $-2x - 5 - 8 - 3x$

1983 $-1 - 3x + 5 - 6x$

1984 $8 + x - 5 + 6x$

1985 $2x - 9x + 9 + 7$

1986 $9x + 4 - 3 - x + 7x$

SUMMER MATH SUCCESS

Name: ______________ Class: __________

Simplifying Expressions

1987 $-5x - 2 + 9x$

1988 $-8 - 8x + 8x - 8 + 8x$

1989 $6x + 8 - x - 3 + 7x - 8$

1990 $7x + 1 + 7x + 3 + 3x + 4$

1991 $-x + 2x$

1992 $-4x + 8 - 8x$

1993 $x + 4 + 6x$

SUMMER MATH SUCCESS

Name: ____________ Class: ____________

Simplifying Expressions

1994 $x + 4 + 7x$

1995 $9x + 4 - 6x + 3 + 2x + 5$

1996 $8 + x - 1 + 5x$

1997 $3 + 6x + 8 + 5x$

1998 $2x - 2 + 3x - 9 + 3x + 7$

1999 $7 - 6x + 9 - 6x + 1 - 8x$

2000 $-5x + 2 - 4x$

SUMMER MATH SUCCESS

Name: ____________ Class: ________

Simplifying Expressions

2001 $-6x + x$

2002 $7x + 3 + x$

2003 $8 + 6x + 6 + 9x$

2004 $-2 + 3 - 8x + 3x - 6 + 7x$

2005 $2 + 3(6x - 2)$

2006 $5x - 8x$

2007 $6x + 1 - 3x + 8 + 6x + 9$

SUMMER MATH SUCCESS

Name: ____________ Class: ________

Inequalities - Addition and Subtraction

Solve.

2008 $5 \leq x - 3$

2009 $8 \geq 1 + x$

2010 $5 < 2 + x$

2011 $7 \leq x - 2$

2012 $x + 1 < 3$

2013 $x - 7 < 9$

SUMMER MATH SUCCESS

Name: ____________________ Class: __________

Inequalities - Addition and Subtraction

Solve.

2014 $9 > x - 8$

2015 $5 > x + 8$

2016 $1 - x \leq 8$

2017 $x + 7 > 1$

2018 $7 \leq 1 + x$

2019 $7 < x - 3$

SUMMER MATH SUCCESS

Name: ____________ Class: ________

Inequalities - Addition and Subtraction

Solve.

2020 $4 - x < 8$

2021 $x + 3 \geq 8$

2022 $2 < 1 + x$

2023 $8 < 5 - x$

2024 $2 - x < 6$

2025 $6 > x + 8$

SUMMER MATH SUCCESS

Name: ________________ Class: __________

Inequalities - Multiplication and Division

Solve.

2026 $4 > 8x$

2027 $6 \leq \frac{x}{5}$

2028 $8 \geq \frac{x}{4}$

2029 $6 \leq 18x$

2030 $8 > \frac{x}{7}$

2031 $2x \leq 5$

SUMMER MATH SUCCESS

Name: ____________ Class: ________

Inequalities - Multiplication and Division

Solve.

2032 $\frac{x}{3} \leq 1$

2033 $6x \geq 10$

2034 $7 \geq \frac{x}{3}$

2035 $12 > 9x$

2036 $7 > \frac{x}{7}$

2037 $4x \geq 2$

SUMMER MATH SUCCESS

Name: ____________ Class: ________

Inequalities - Multiplication and Division

Solve.

2038 $\frac{x}{2} \geq 6$

2039 $5 \leq 3x$

2040 $\frac{x}{2} < 1$

2041 $4x < 8$

2042 $3 \leq 4x$

2043 $\frac{x}{7} \leq 6$

SUMMER MATH SUCCESS

Name: ________________ Class: __________

Find the Area and Perimeter

2044

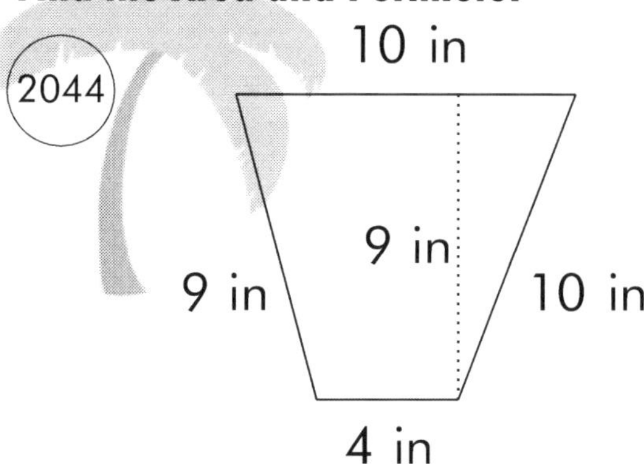

____

2045

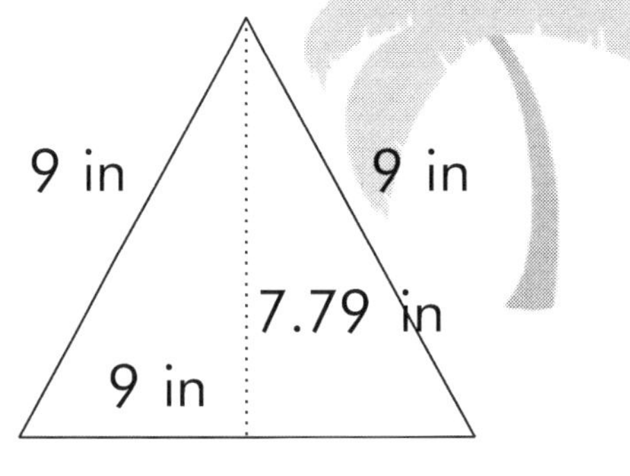

____

2046

4 in

13 in

16 in

____

2047

4 in

9 in

6 in

8 in

____

2048

15 in

14 in

13.95 in

6 in

____

2049

15 in

11 in

11 in

____

SUMMER
MATH SUCCESS

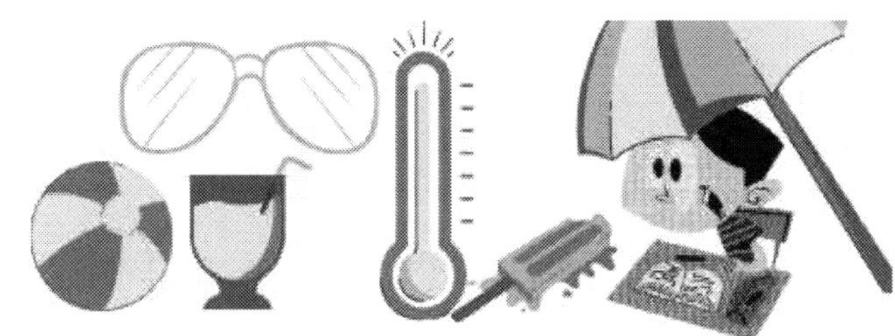

Name: ____________________ Class: __________

Find the Area and Perimeter

2050

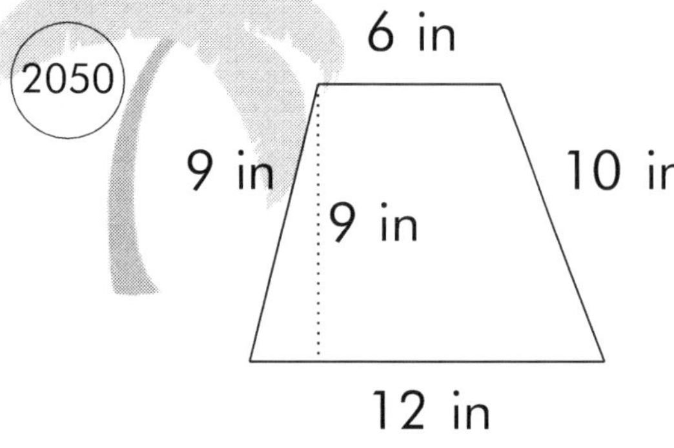

____

2051

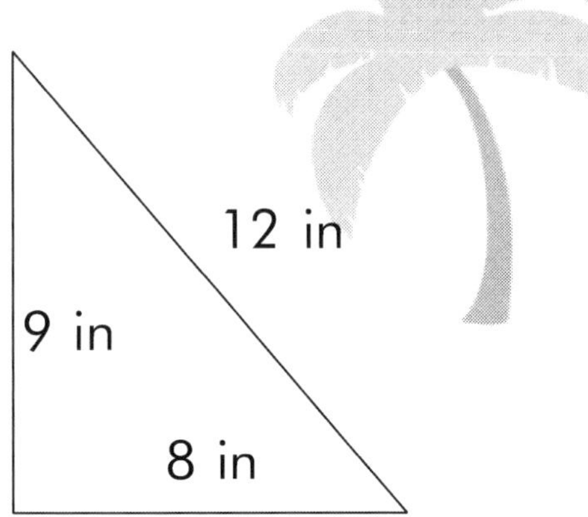

____

2052

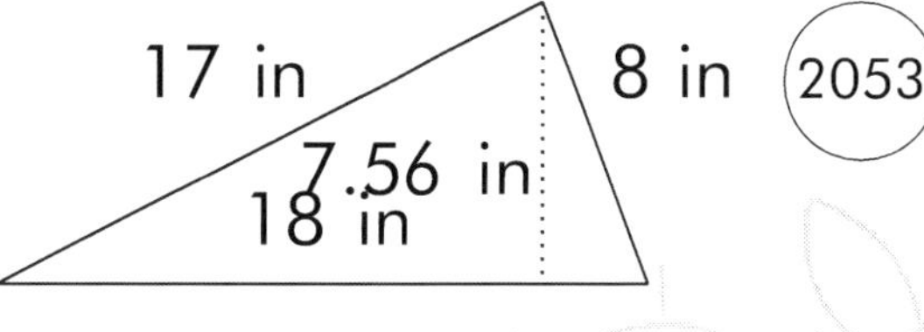

____

2053

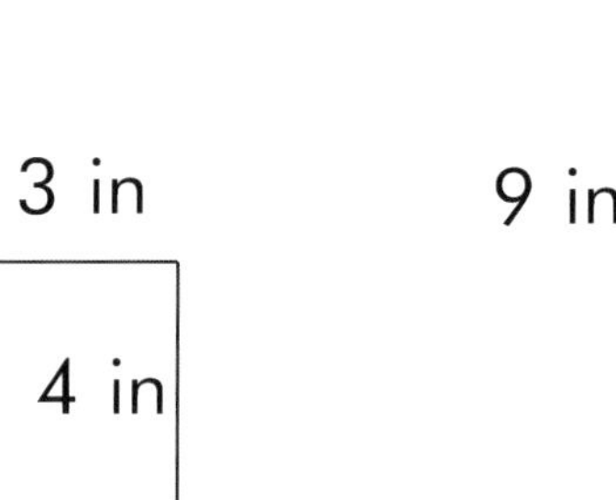

____

2054

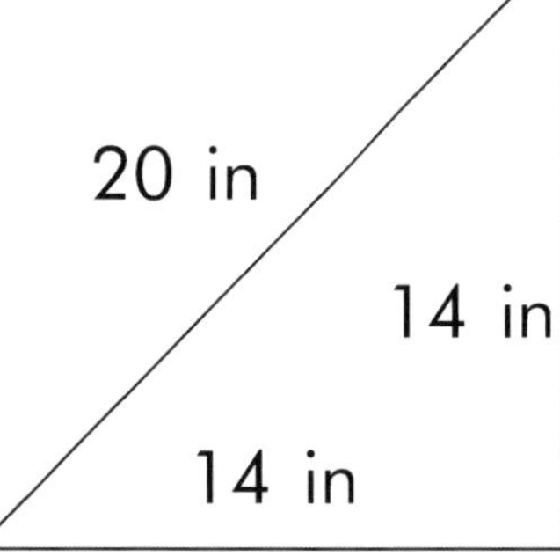

____

2055

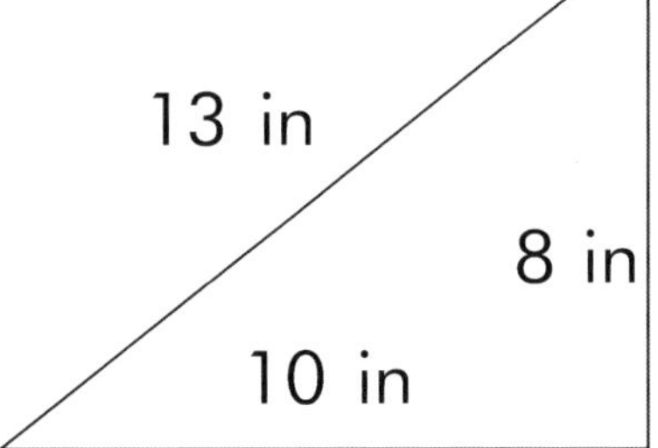

____

SUMMER MATH SUCCESS

Name: ____________ Class: ________

Find the Area and Perimeter

2056

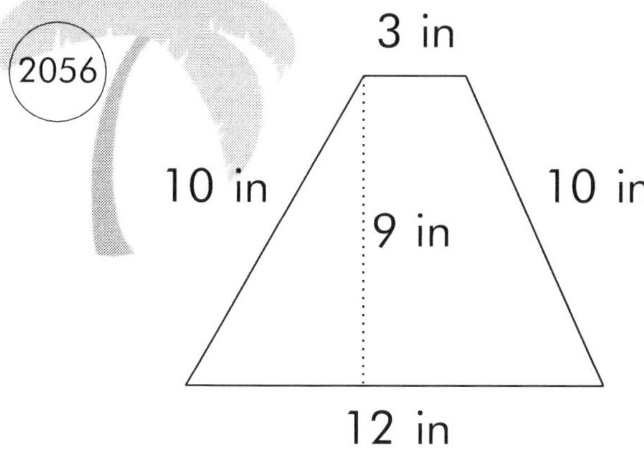

____

2057

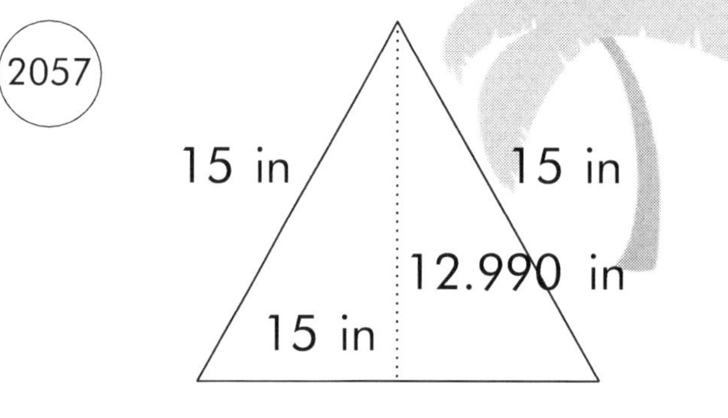

____

2058

2059

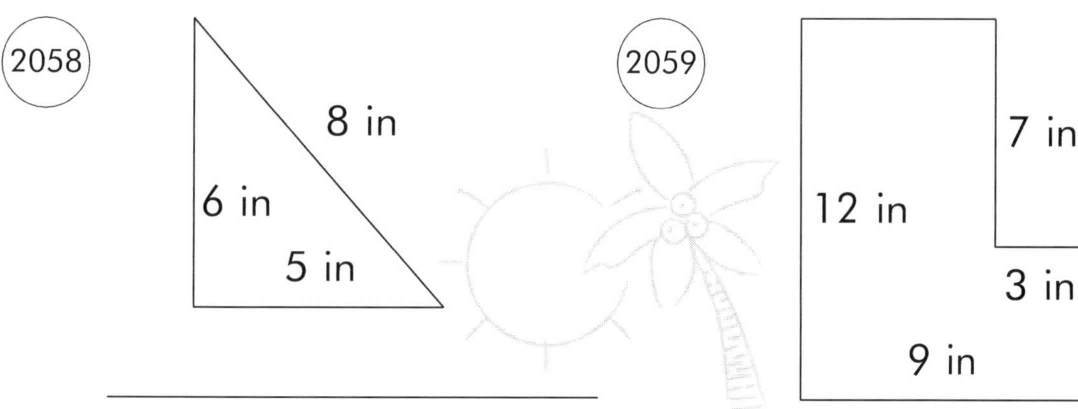

____

____

2060

2061

____

____

SUMMER MATH SUCCESS

Name: ________________ Class: __________

Find the Volume and Surfrace Area

2062

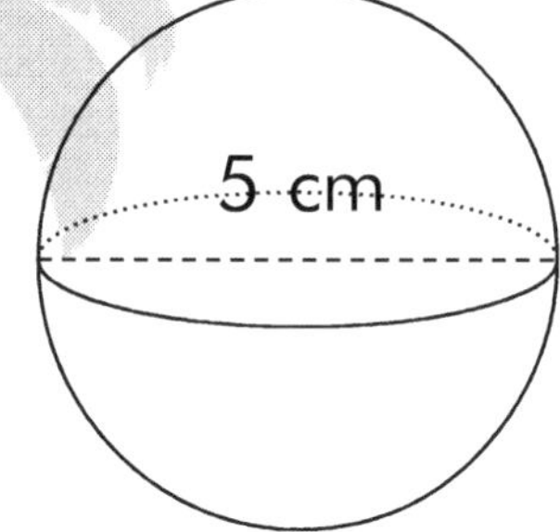

2063

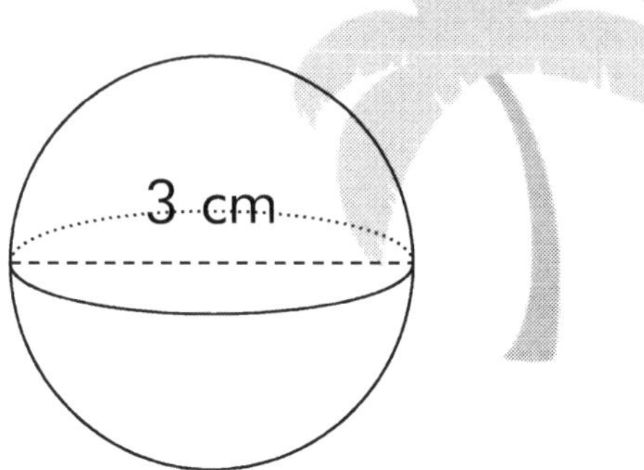

2064

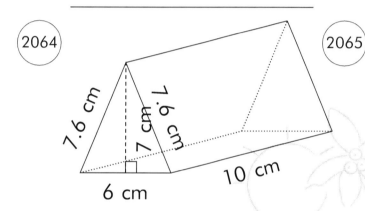

7.6 cm
7.6 cm
7 cm
6 cm
10 cm

2065

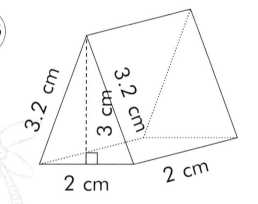

3.2 cm
3.2 cm
3 cm
2 cm
2 cm

2066

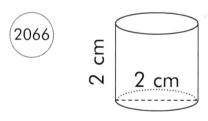

2 cm
2 cm

2067

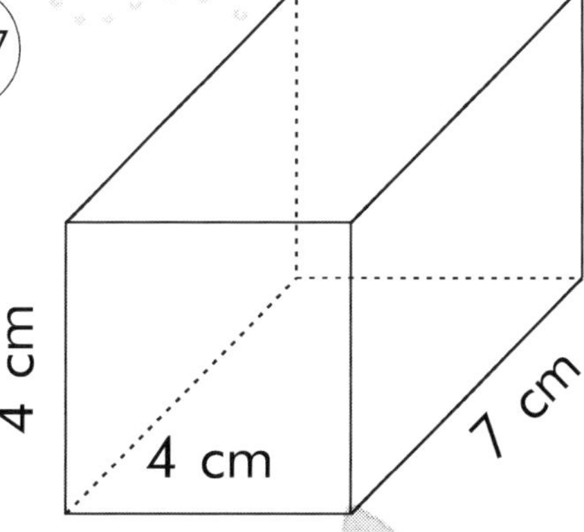

SUMMER MATH SUCCESS

Name: ________________ Class: __________

Find the Volume and Surfrace Area

2068

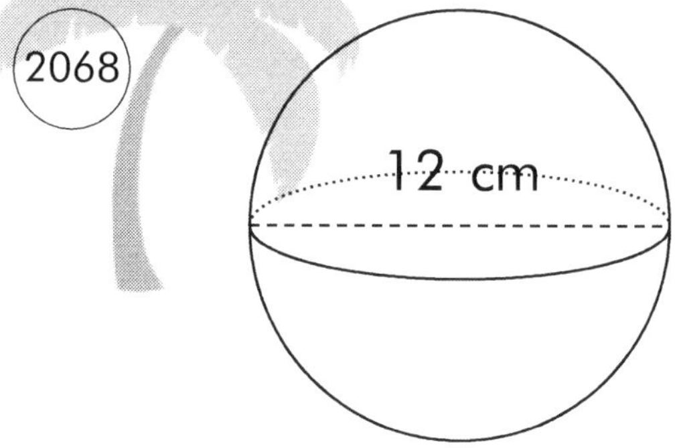

2069

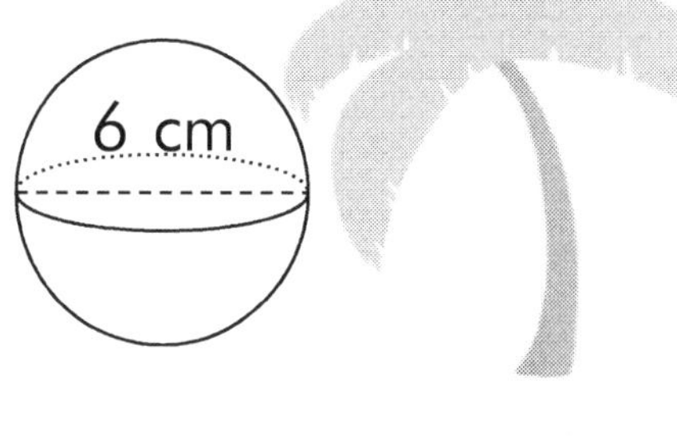

2070

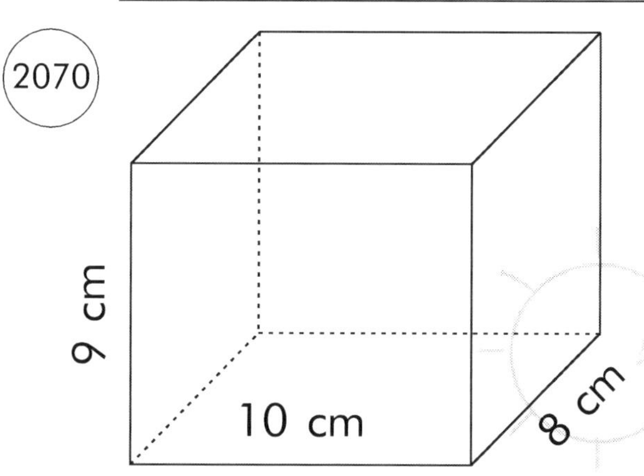

2071

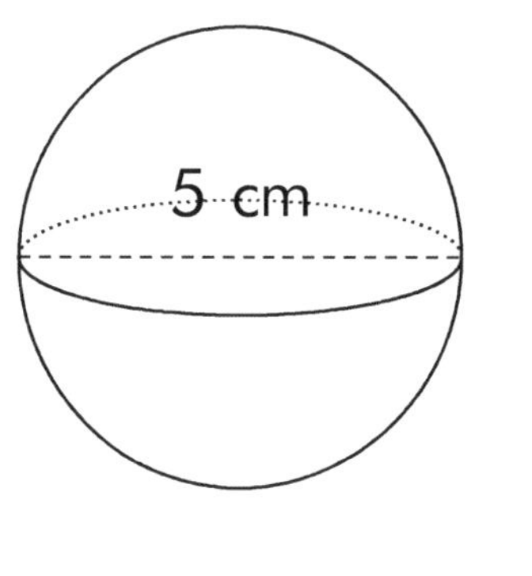

2072

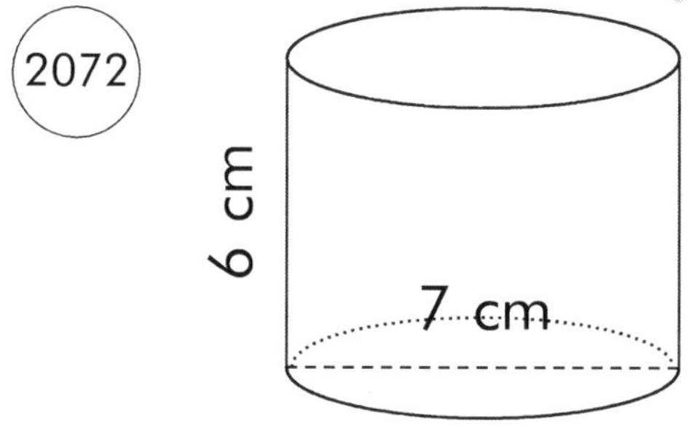

2073

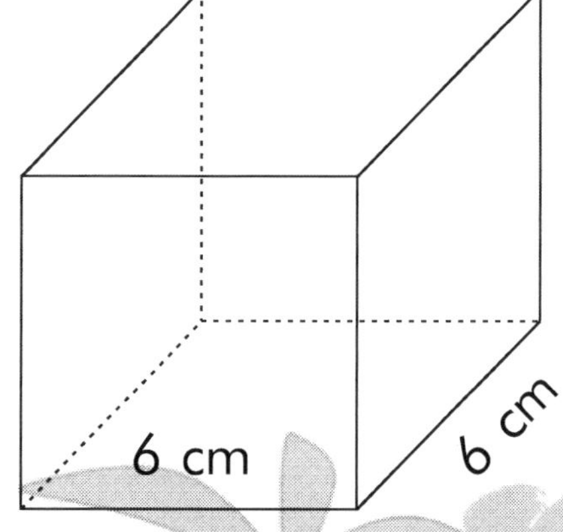

SUMMER MATH SUCCESS

Name: ____________ Class: ____________

Find the Volume and Surfrace Area

2074

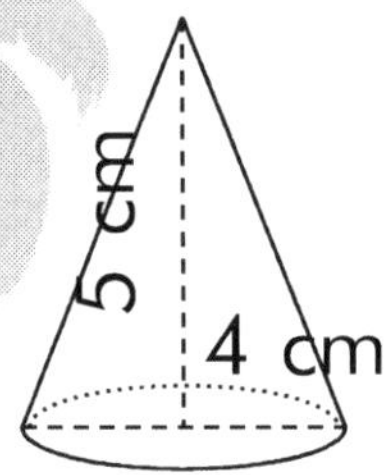

____

2075

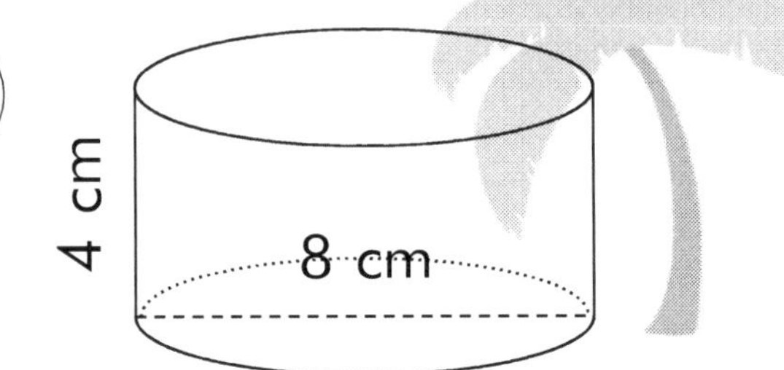

____

2076

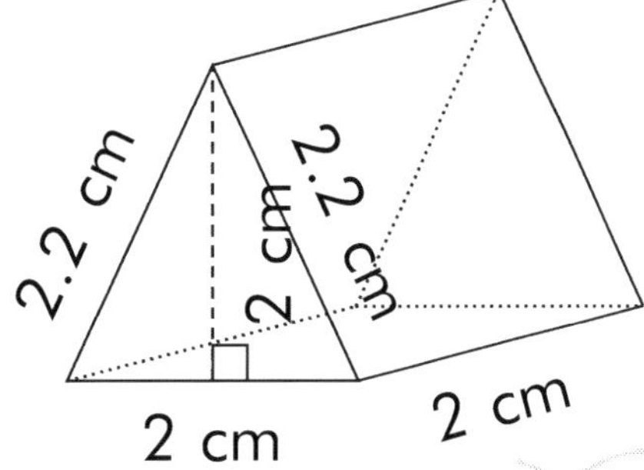

____

2077

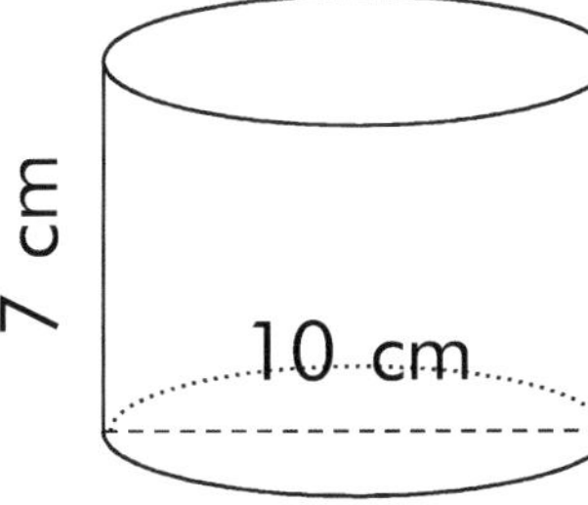

____

2078

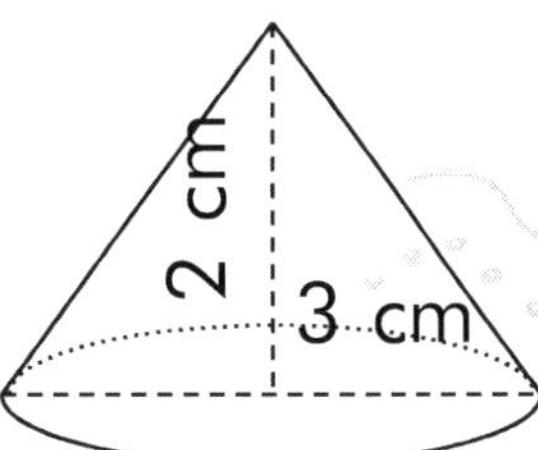

____

2079

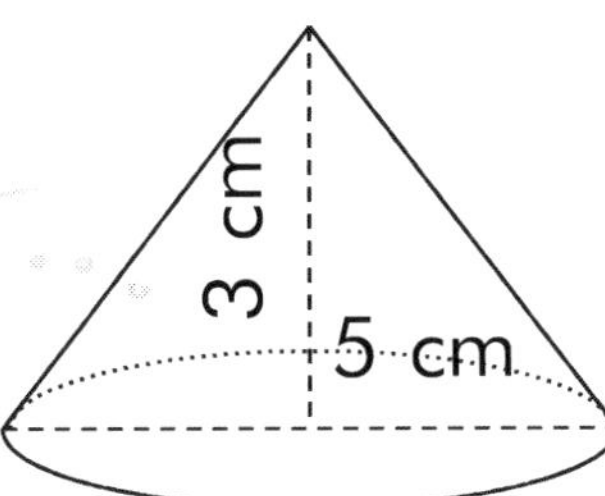

____

SUMMER MATH SUCCESS

Name: ____________________ Class: ___________

Calculate the area of each circle.

2080

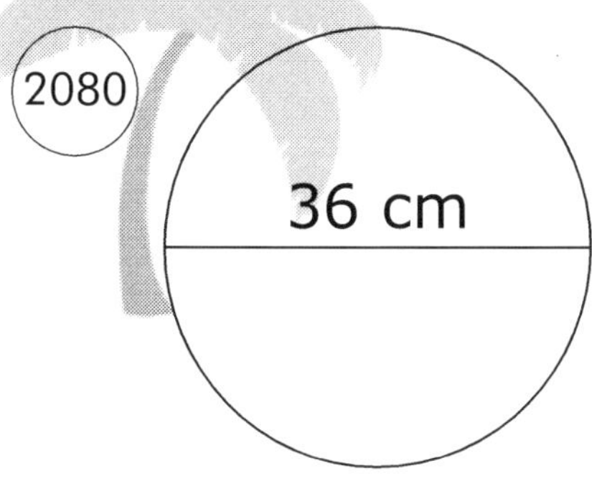

36 cm

____

2081

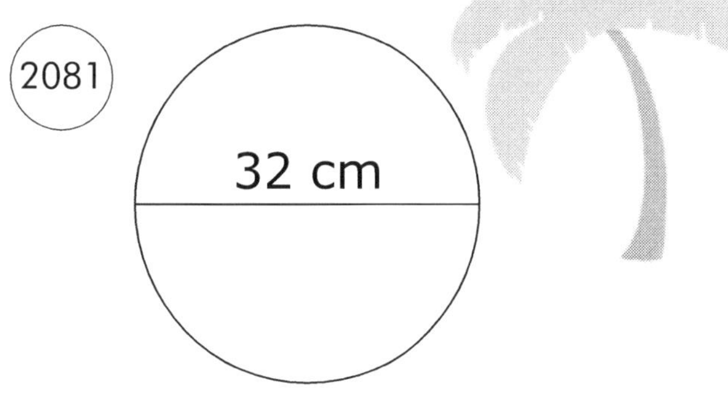

32 cm

____

2082

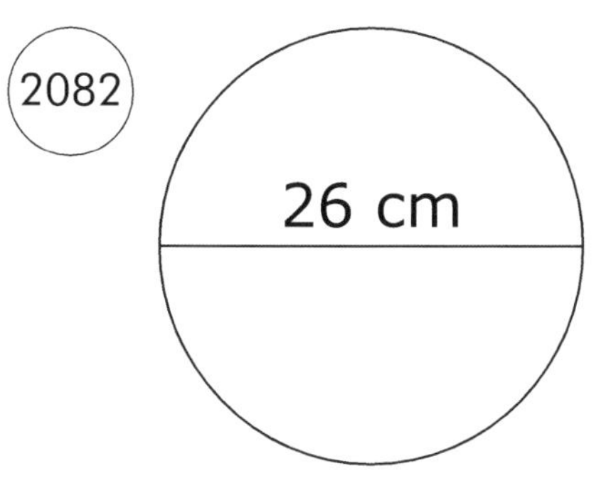

26 cm

____

2083

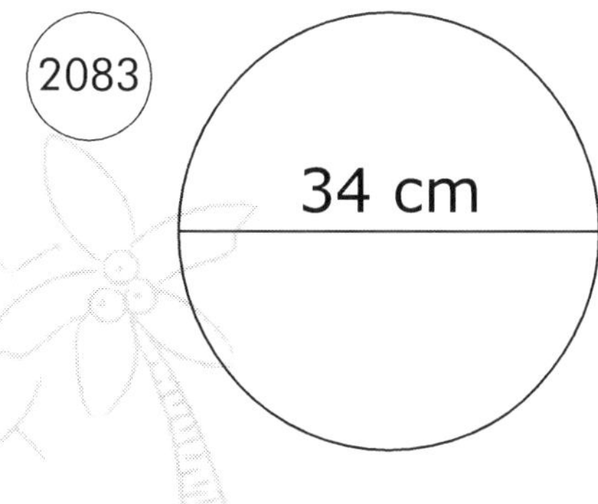

34 cm

____

2084

28 cm

____

2085

18 cm

____

SUMMER MATH SUCCESS

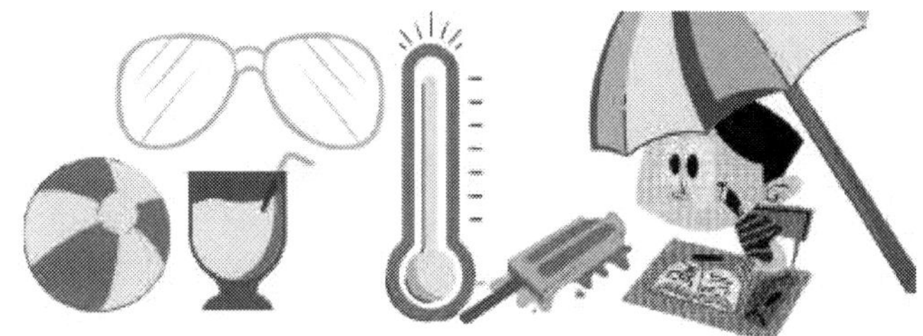

Name: ____________________ Class: __________

Calculate the area of each circle.

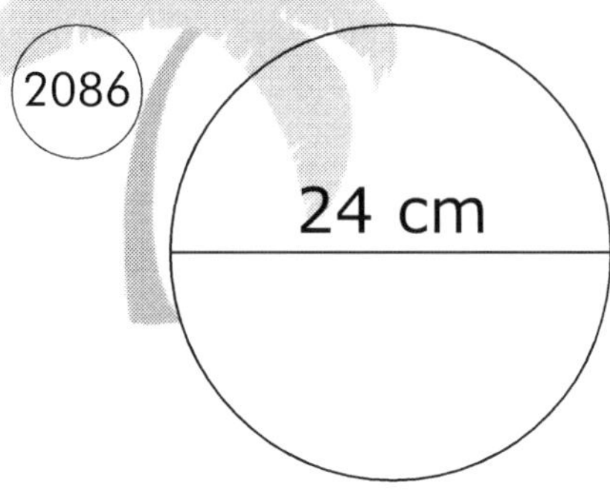

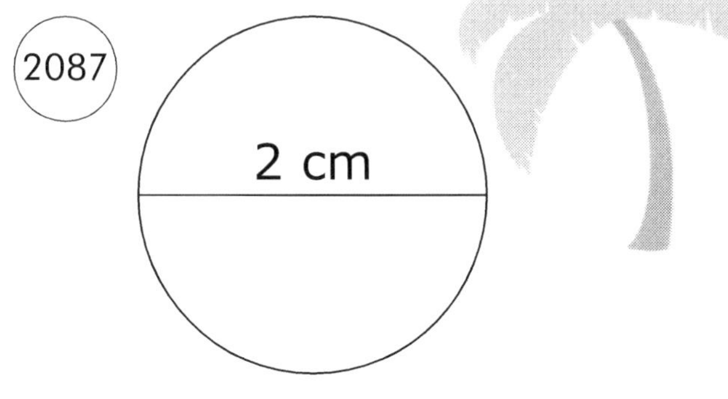

2086 24 cm

____

2087 2 cm

____

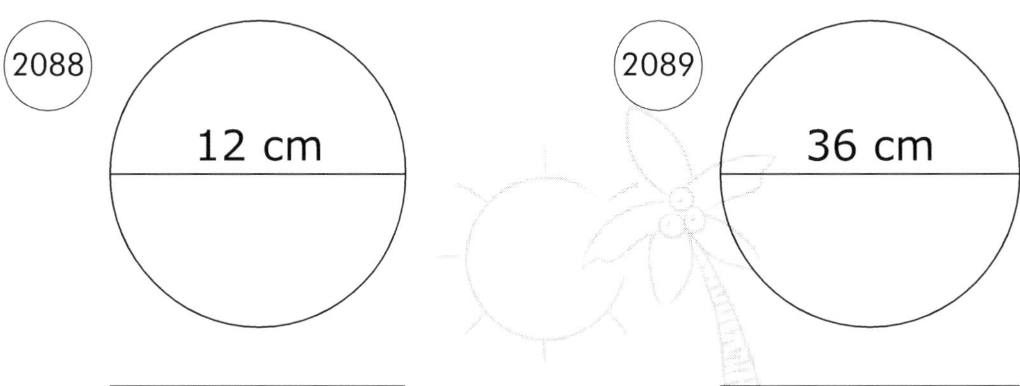

2088 12 cm

____

2089 36 cm

____

2090 10 cm

____

2091 16 cm

____

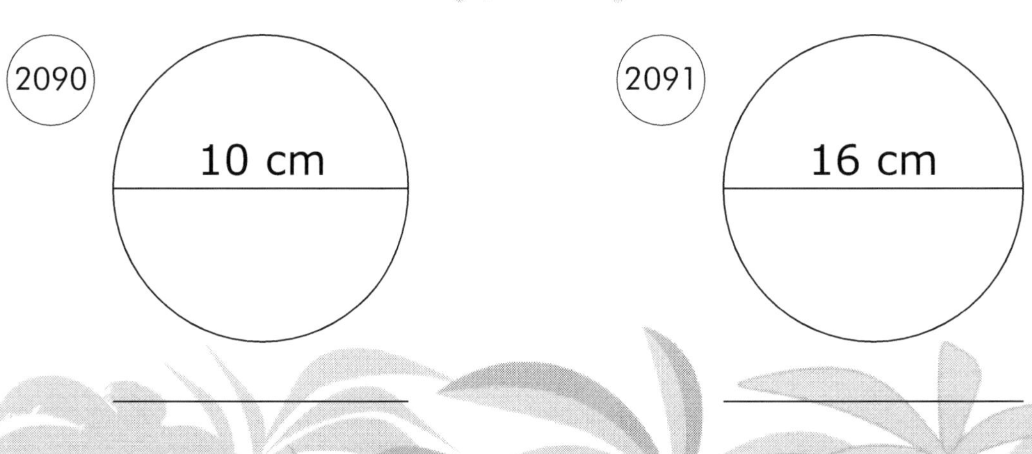

SUMMER MATH SUCCESS

Name: ________________ Class: __________

Calculate the area of each circle.

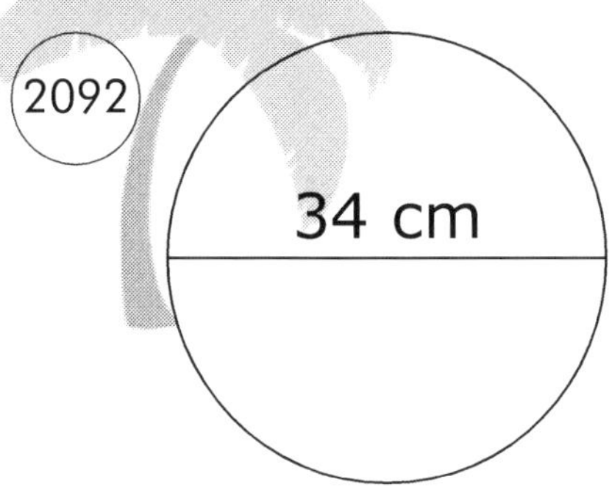

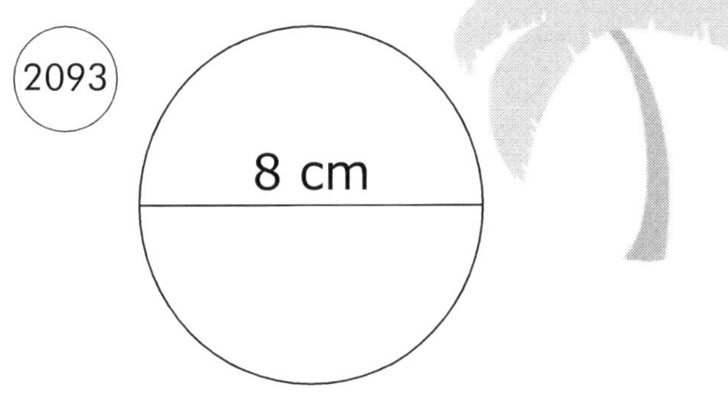

2092

34 cm

____

2093

8 cm

____

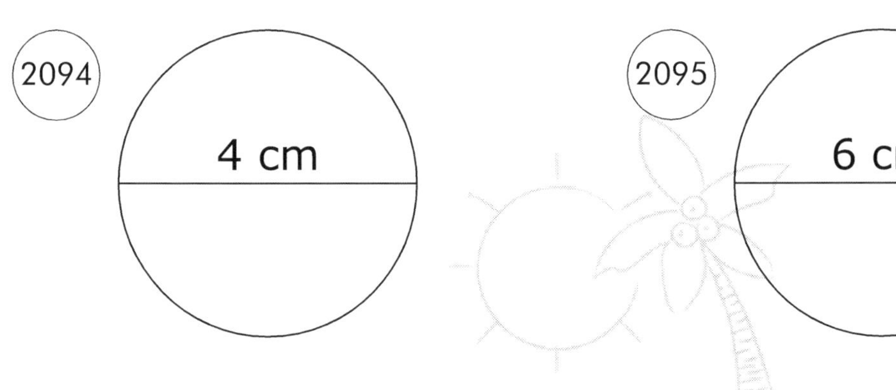

2094

4 cm

____

2095

6 cm

____

2096

36 cm

____

2097

40 cm

____

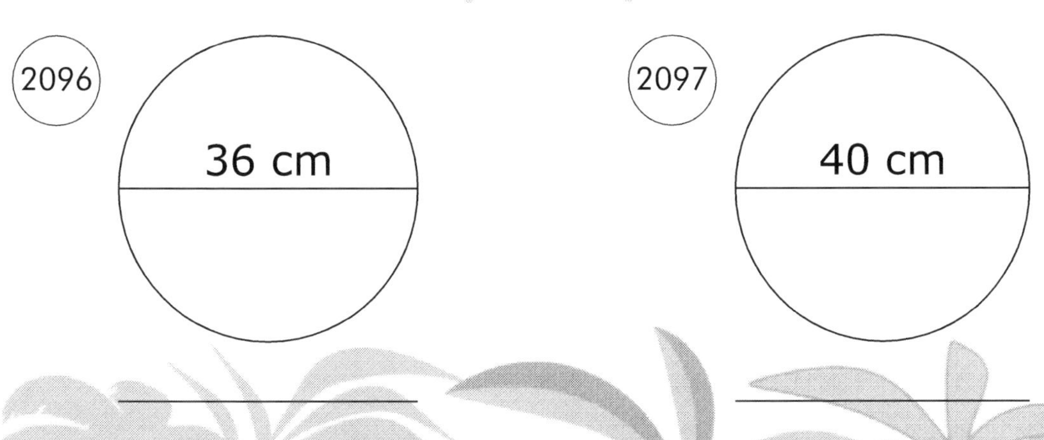

SUMMER MATH SUCCESS

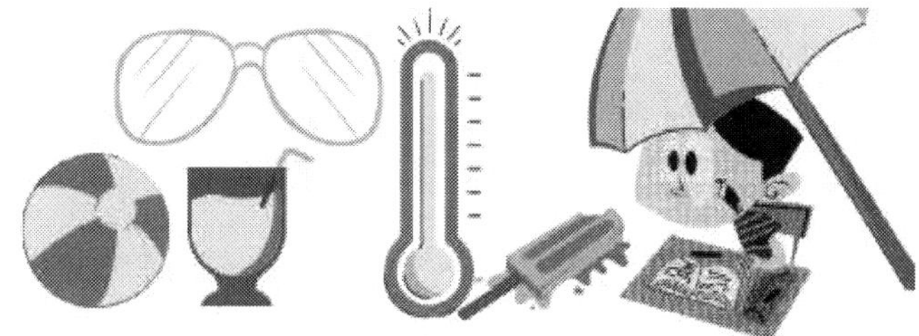

Name: ____________________ Class: __________

Calculate the circumference of each circle.

2098 — 38 cm

____

2099 — 2 cm

____

2100 — 12 cm

____

2101 — 24 cm

____

2102 — 10 cm

____

2103 — 22 cm

____

SUMMER MATH SUCCESS

Name: ____________ Class: ________

Calculate the circumference of each circle.

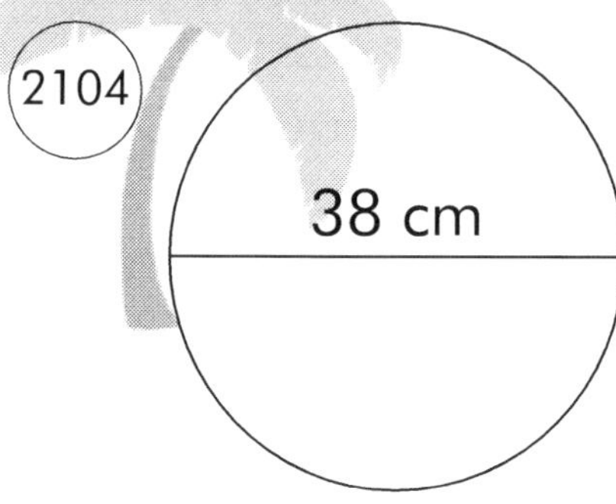
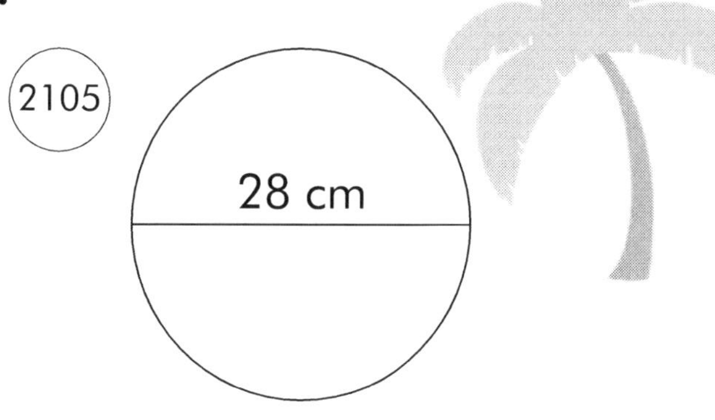

2104 38 cm

____

2105 28 cm

____

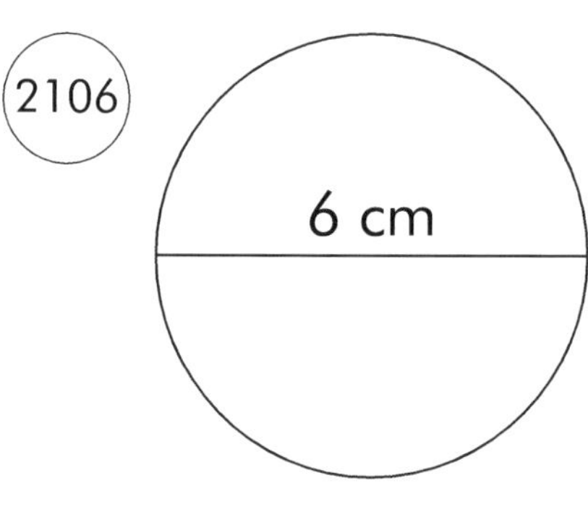
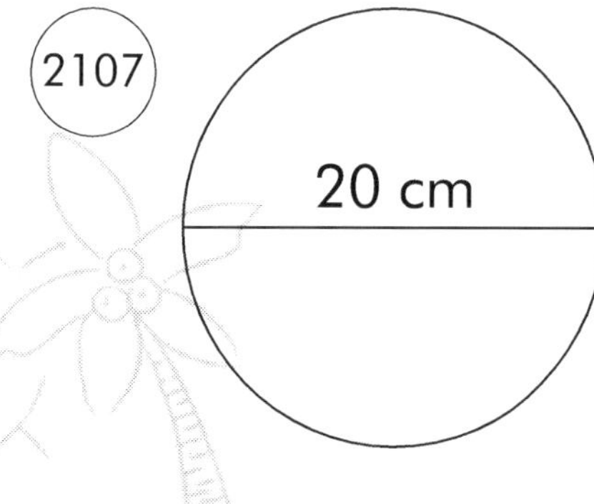

2106 6 cm

____

2107 20 cm

____

2108 4 cm

____

2109 12 cm

____

SUMMER MATH SUCCESS

Name: ____________ Class: ________

Calculate the circumference of each circle.

2110
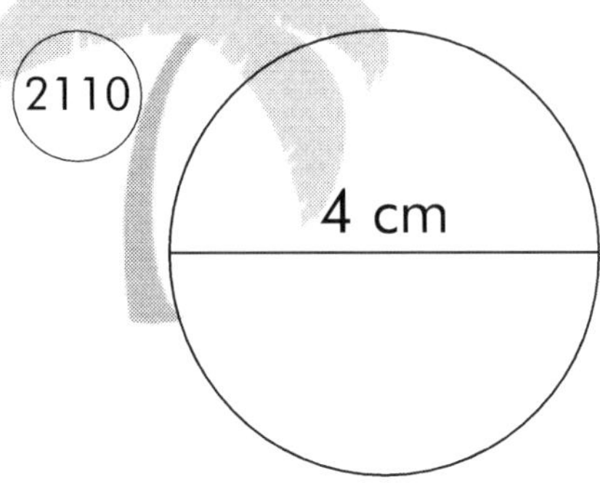

4 cm

____

2111
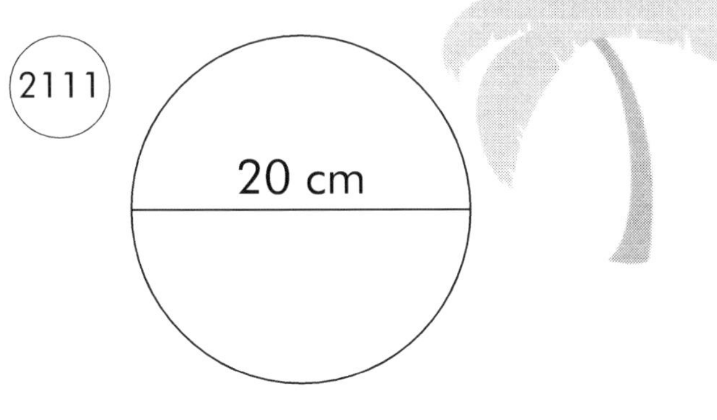

20 cm

____

2112
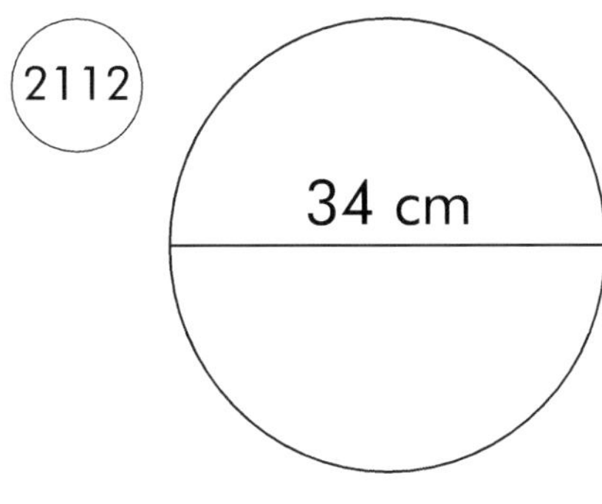

34 cm

____

2113
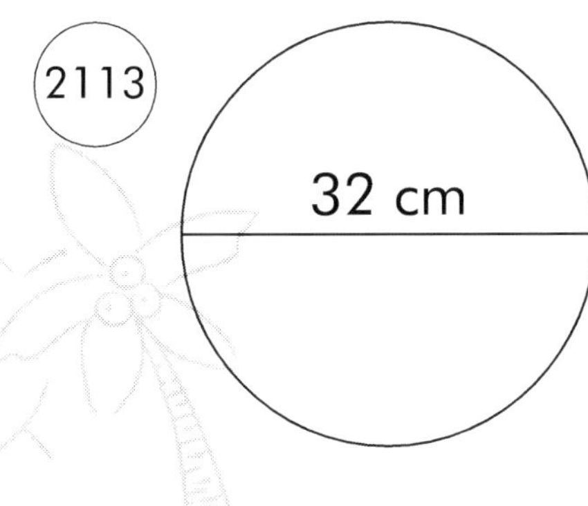

32 cm

____

2114

2 cm

____

2115

6 cm

____

SUMMER
MATH SUCCESS

Name: ____________ Class: ________

Measure of Center - Mean

Find the Mean of the following sets of data.

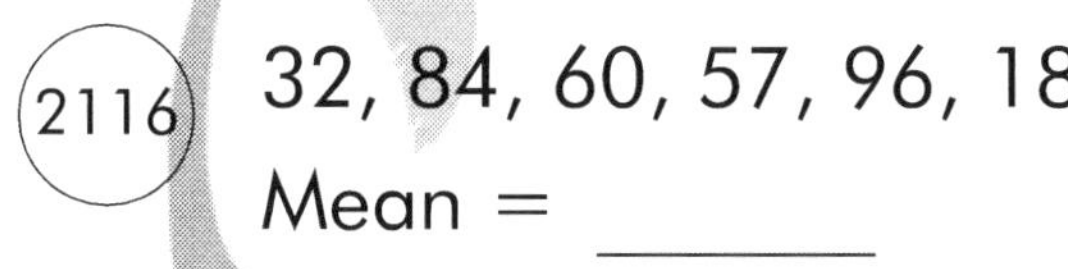

2116 32, 84, 60, 57, 96, 18

Mean = ______

2117 28, 80, 58, 77, 91, 96, 30, 71

Mean = ______

2118 24, 68, 57, 2, 87, 41, 44

Mean = ______

2119 48, 49, 14, 96, 14, 15, 7, 48, 66

Mean = ______

2120 27, 91, 85, 53, 74, 49, 52

Mean = ______

2121 72, 21, 95, 39, 35, 55, 99, 17, 61

Mean = ______

SUMMER MATH SUCCESS

Name: ______________ Class: ________

Measure of Center - Mean

Find the Mean of the following sets of data.

2122 38, 25, 35, 67, 45, 14, 32
Mean = ______

2123 6, 83, 83, 36, 47, 60, 82, 4, 22
Mean = ____

2124 32, 92, 51, 99, 12, 76, 97, 74
Mean = ______

2125 16, 84, 81, 91, 3, 10, 92, 49
Mean = _____

2126 96, 36, 76, 89, 71, 80
Mean = ______

2127 21, 13, 59, 79, 70, 91, 14
Mean = ______

SUMMER MATH SUCCESS

Name: ____________ Class: ________

Measure of Center - Median

Find the Median of the following sets of data.

2128) 6, 12, 38, 92, 17, 3, 63
Median = ___

2129) 49, 17, 50, 61, 28, 61, 51
Median = ___

2130) 61, 33, 41, 4, 73, 90, 86
Median = ___

2131) 50, 25, 6, 14, 50, 52, 71, 38
Median = ___

2132) 41, 32, 7, 6, 60, 10, 72, 43, 99
Median = ___

2133) 85, 8, 30, 1, 79, 85, 16, 62
Median = ___

SUMMER
MATH SUCCESS

Name: ________ Class: ________

Measure of Center - Median
Find the Median of the following sets of data.

2134 11, 29, 60, 80, 19, 76, 96, 1
Median = ____

2135 28, 55, 87, 33, 79, 66, 51, 91
Median = ____

2136 11, 76, 19, 54, 22, 2, 41
Median = ____

2137 88, 89, 42, 18, 66, 61, 86, 70, 40
Median = ____

2138 90, 51, 40, 23, 12, 58, 23, 55
Median = ____

2139 11, 6, 32, 54, 85, 11, 20
Median = ____

SUMMER
MATH SUCCESS

Name: ____________ Class: ________

Measure of Center - Mode

Find the Mode of the following sets of data.

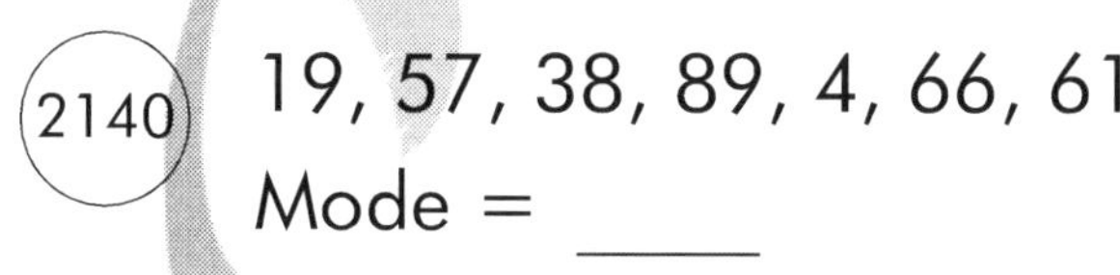

2140 19, 57, 38, 89, 4, 66, 61
Mode = ____

2141 41, 10, 87, 71, 90, 77, 58, 30
Mode = ____

2142 40, 41, 85, 48, 42, 28, 27
Mode = ____

2143 28, 80, 52, 53, 63, 43, 17, 69
Mode = ____

2144 86, 4, 79, 22, 99, 10, 23, 96, 67
Mode = ____

2145 73, 29, 11, 30, 35, 40
Mode = ____

SUMMER MATH SUCCESS

Name: ____________ Class: ________

Measure of Center - Mode

Find the Mode of the following sets of data.

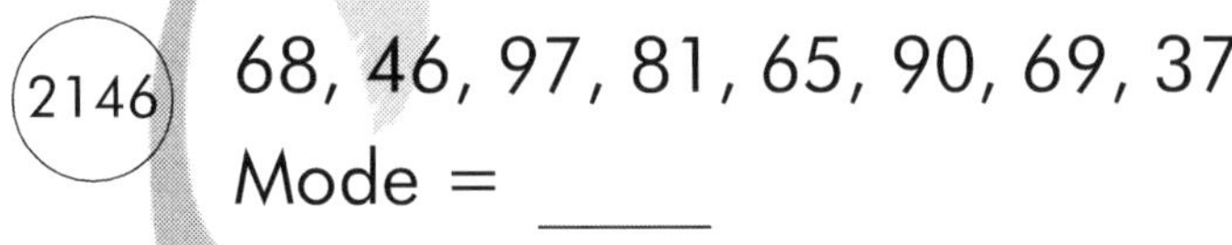

2146 68, 46, 97, 81, 65, 90, 69, 37
Mode = ____

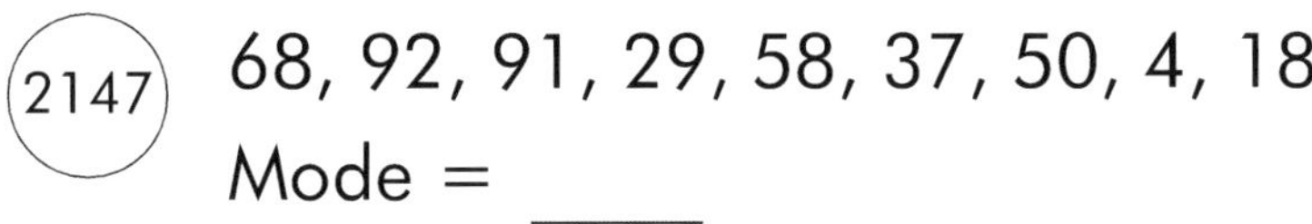

2147 68, 92, 91, 29, 58, 37, 50, 4, 18
Mode = ____

2148 25, 41, 1, 68, 12, 55, 59, 20
Mode = ____

2149 18, 45, 18, 75, 14, 18, 96, 93, 40
Mode = ____

2150 84, 8, 66, 62, 51, 78, 18, 66
Mode = ____

2151 11, 29, 8, 81, 65, 59, 18, 70
Mode = ____

SUMMER MATH SUCCESS

Name: ____________ Class: ________

Measure of Variability - Range

Find the Range of the following sets of data.

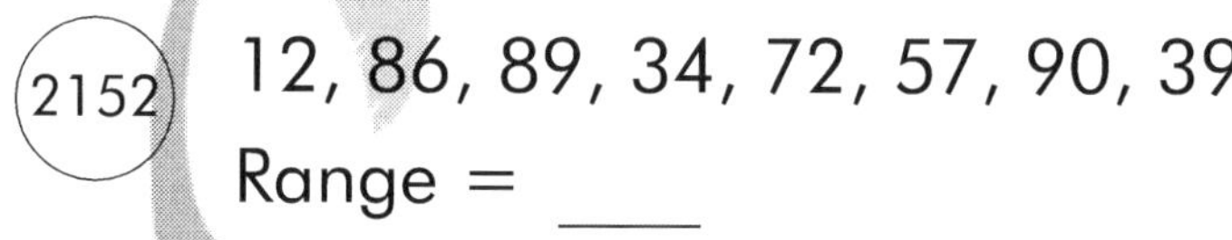

(2152) 12, 86, 89, 34, 72, 57, 90, 39

Range = ____

(2153) 61, 48, 46, 52, 62, 55, 75, 94

Range = ____

(2154) 35, 19, 53, 42, 37, 55, 73, 62, 83

Range = ____

(2155) 2, 1, 27, 51, 39, 52, 85

Range = ____

(2156) 1, 5, 2, 32, 8, 59

Range = ____

(2157) 67, 28, 18, 28, 2, 4

Range = ____

SUMMER MATH SUCCESS

Name: ____________ Class: ________

Measure of Variability - Range

Find the Range of the following sets of data.

2158 32, 65, 5, 56, 54, 13

Range = ____

2159 46, 46, 7, 75, 33, 56, 13, 27

Range = ____

2160 50, 71, 57, 64, 87, 22, 95, 61, 51

Range = ____

2161 57, 53, 44, 87, 76, 51, 26, 25, 10

Range = ____

2162 54, 69, 31, 19, 97, 44

Range = ____

2163 72, 39, 93, 7, 78, 25, 72, 46, 19

Range = ____

SUMMER MATH SUCCESS

Name: ____________ Class: ________

ANSWERS

Page 1: Multiplication with Whole Numbers

1. 1 1/3	2. 1	3. 7 1/5	4. 4	5. 1 1/2	6. 1 1/4
7. 1 3/5	8. 1	9. 2	10. 2/3	11. 5 1/4	12. 1 3/5
13. 3 3/4	14. 4	15. 1 1/3	16. 2 1/4	17. 5 1/4	18. 3 1/2
19. 4/5	20. 4 2/3				

Page 2: Multiplication with Whole Numbers

21. 1 2/5	22. 2 1/3	23. 4 3/8	24. 2	25. 5 1/3	26. 1/2
27. 2 1/4	28. 1 1/3	29. 7 1/5	30. 2	31. 4 1/2	32. 1 2/3
33. 4	34. 1	35. 3	36. 4	37. 3 1/2	38. 2
39. 2/5	40. 2 2/3				

Page 3: Multiplication with Whole Numbers

41. 2 1/2	42. 2 2/3	43. 1 1/2	44. 6	45. 4	46. 6 1/8
47. 1 1/2	48. 5 1/3	49. 1	50. 1/2	51. 1 2/5	52. 4
53. 2 1/2	54. 1 1/3	55. 6	56. 5	57. 1	58. 3 1/2
59. 1 3/4	60. 1				

Page 4: Division with Whole Numbers

61. 1/3	62. 1/18	63. 1/12	64. 7/24	65. 1/12	66. 1/20
67. 1/24	68. 3/4	69. 1/6	70. 1/40	71. 1/12	72. 1/6
73. 1/12	74. 2/5	75. 3/16	76. 1/12	77. 1/12	78. 3/4
79. 2/15	80. 2/3				

Page 5: Division with Whole Numbers

81. 2/25	82. 1/4	83. 1/15	84. 1/8	85. 2/21	86. 1/3
87. 1/4	88. 1/6	89. 1/12	90. 1/12	91. 1/21	92. 1/35

SUMMER MATH SUCCESS

Name: ____________ Class: ________

93. 3/20 94. 2/27 95. 1/27 96. 1/12 97. 1/16 98. 2/21
99. 1/21 100. 1/5

Page 6: Division with Whole Numbers

101. 3/40 102. 1/2 103. 1/8 104. 1/48 105. 1/15 106. 1/3
107. 1/15 108. 1/4 109. 1/9 110. 5/36 111. 3/20 112. 1/12
113. 2/3 114. 3/20 115. 3/20 116. 1/14 117. 1/16 118. 1/45
119. 1/12 120. 1/24

Page 7: Mixed Fractions - Multiplication

121. 14 2/7 122. 11 8/17 123. 8 13/76
124. 25 3/10 125. 7 245/368 126. 56 2/9
127. 61 3/50 128. 6 5/104 129. 15 11/15
130. 18 3/25

Page 8: Mixed Fractions - Multiplication

131. 32 173/176 132. 40 232/575 133. 36 17/180
134. 22 13/21 135. 15 1/2 136. 43 83/350
137. 14 34/39 138. 12 1/2 139. 5 31/1000
140. 80 284/375

Page 9: Mixed Fractions - Multiplication

141. 38 269/1100 142. 71 169/180 143. 41 9/28
144. 82 15/64 145. 24 46/75 146. 9 37/130
147. 15 8/21 148. 28 59/190 149. 19 49/384
150. 58 3/4

Page 10: Mixed Fractions- Division

151. 1121/1200 152. 1017/1184 153. 1175/1568

SUMMER MATH SUCCESS

Name: ________________ Class: __________

154. 182/345
155. 1 47/243
156. 1 151/400
157. 1900/2191
158. 1 19/280
159. 1 1039/1686
160. 114/245

Page 11: Mixed Fractions- Division

161. 175/396
162. 63/110
163. 83/86
164. 2 79/500
165. 1 53/110
166. 1 17/66
167. 1 9/56
168. 2 227/588
169. 185/412
170. 3 1242/1411

Page 12: Mixed Fractions- Division

171. 7 21/52
172. 460/2889
173. 99/128
174. 71/154
175. 51/100
176. 1 1042/1183
177. 174/187
178. 2831/3200
179. 256/625
180. 4 23/24

Page 13: Fractions: Multiple Operations

181. 5
182. 8/9
183. 2 1/2
184. 2
185. 15/512
186. 1 1/2
187. 1 4/5
188. 1 1/8
189. 2 9/20
190. 3/4

Page 14: Fractions: Multiple Operations

191. 1/3
192. 7/8
193. 1 7/16
194. 1 2/5
195. 2/5
196. 1/4
197. 93/100
198. 0
199. 5/9
200. 1 1/4

Page 15: Fractions: Multiple Operations

201. 9/10
202. 1 3/8
203. 24/125
204. 1 1/6
205. 11/16
206. 1 1/5
207. 9/10
208. 31/36

SUMMER MATH SUCCESS

Name: ______________ Class: ________

209. 7/25 210. 5/8

Page 16: Fractions: Multiple Operations

211. 1/216 212. 31/36 213. 4 7/8 214. 15/16 215. 3/64

216. 5 217. 5 7/15 218. 59/64 219. 1 1/3 220. 49/80

Page 17: Fractions: Multiple Operations

221. 6/25 222. 1 223. 13/16 224. 3/5 225. 1/216

226. 2/3 227. 2 1/5 228. 2 2/5 229. 1/2 230. 1 2/3

Page 18: Fractions: Multiple Operations

231. 1/24 232. 4/9 233. 7/16 234. 5 13/24

235. 1/6 236. 4 237. 5/18 238. 1 1/3

239. 5/6 240. 1/3

Page 19: Fractions: Multiple Operations

241. 2/3 242. 1 1/4 243. 19/25 244. 3/16

245. 6 5/6 246. 3/8 247. 3/64 248. 245/512

249. 5 1/6 250. 10 3/8

Page 20: Fractions: Multiple Operations

251. 35/36 252. 1 1/2 253. 1/2 254. 23/48 255. 7 4/5

256. 1/3 257. 25/64 258. 1/9 259. 7/36 260. 0

Page 21: Fractions: Multiple Operations

261. 1/2 262. 15/16 263. 7/10 264. 13/16 265. 13/18

266. 1 1/2 267. 2 268. 2 269. 2 270. 1/6

Page 22: Fractions: Multiple Operations

271. 9 1/2 272. 1 1/3 273. 5/8 274. 8 1/15 275. 8/9

276. 5/32 277. 7/9 278. 3/4 279. 2/9 280. 11/36

SUMMER MATH SUCCESS

Name: ____________ Class: ________

Page 23: Simplifying Fractions

281. 7 1/15	**282.** 6 1/5	**283.** 6/7	**284.** 1/3	**285.** 7
286. 8 1/2	**287.** 9	**288.** 1/3	**289.** 4 9/10	**290.** 9
291. 2/5	**292.** 1/2	**293.** 2 6/7	**294.** 7	**295.** 6
296. 7 2/15	**297.** 9	**298.** 5/6	**299.** 8 1/14	**300.** 2/5

Page 24: Simplifying Fractions

301. 2	**302.** 5 1/6	**303.** 6 2/3	**304.** 5	**305.** 7
306. 3 2/3	**307.** 4	**308.** 3	**309.** 8 1/4	**310.** 1/6
311. 7 2/5	**312.** 8 2/3	**313.** 3/4	**314.** 1/12	**315.** 2
316. 3 3/5	**317.** 6	**318.** 8	**319.** 8	**320.** 3/4

Page 25: Simplifying Fractions

321. 8 1/4	**322.** 7	**323.** 1/3	**324.** 2/5	**325.** 6
326. 3 3/4	**327.** 3/4	**328.** 9/10	**329.** 2 3/5	**330.** 4
331. 11/12	**332.** 5	**333.** 9	**334.** 3/4	**335.** 6
336. 3/4	**337.** 4 3/8	**338.** 2/5	**339.** 5 4/5	**340.** 2

Page 26: Simplifying Fractions

341. 6/7	**342.** 9 1/3	**343.** 4 2/3	**344.** 7	**345.** 7/10
346. 7 1/4	**347.** 11/12	**348.** 7 4/5	**349.** 3	**350.** 6 2/5
351. 3/8	**352.** 8	**353.** 9	**354.** 2 1/14	**355.** 2
356. 9 3/5	**357.** 3 3/10	**358.** 8	**359.** 9	**360.** 5

Page 27: Simplifying Fractions

361. 1/3	**362.** 3 5/14	**363.** 5/6	**364.** 1/2
365. 3 1/4	**366.** 1/10	**367.** 1/2	**368.** 8
369. 7 2/3	**370.** 2 1/3	**371.** 9 14/15	**372.** 1/4

SUMMER
MATH SUCCESS

Name: ______ Class: ______

373. 5	374. 1/2	375. 2/5	376. 2
377. 2/3	378. 4	379. 1/6	380. 3/4

Page 28: Simplifying Fractions

381. 3 6/7	382. 3/4	383. 1/4	384. 9 9/10
385. 2/7	386. 4 1/15	387. 7 3/8	388. 3 1/2
389. 1/2	390. 8 4/5	391. 4	392. 5 2/3
393. 1/4	394. 4	395. 7 3/5	396. 1/8
397. 7	398. 2	399. 4	400. 2 13/14

Page 29: Simplifying Fractions

401. 2/3	402. 2 1/2	403. 3/4	404. 2 2/3	405. 5 4/7
406. 6	407. 8 4/5	408. 3 2/15	409. 7/8	410. 6
411. 6	412. 5 9/10	413. 4	414. 7	415. 4 1/3
416. 8	417. 5 1/4	418. 4 4/5	419. 4 1/2	420. 2

Page 30: Simplifying Fractions

421. 7	422. 3 5/14	423. 8	424. 9	425. 4/5
426. 6	427. 9	428. 1/2	429. 2 2/7	430. 3 3/5
431. 3 2/5	432. 4 2/3	433. 2	434. 3 7/8	435. 2 1/3
436. 6	437. 1/10	438. 1/5	439. 1/2	440. 6 1/12

Page 31: Simplifying Fractions

441. 5	442. 1/3	443. 7	444. 5	445. 2
446. 6 1/2	447. 6 3/4	448. 3 2/7	449. 6	450. 9 4/5
451. 8 1/10	452. 6 2/3	453. 2/3	454. 2/3	455. 6 1/5
456. 6/7	457. 7/12	458. 1/2	459. 2/3	460. 8 1/10

SUMMER MATH SUCCESS

Name: ________________ Class: __________

Page 32: Simplifying Fractions

461. 6 1/4	**462.** 7 2/3	**463.** 6 1/5	**464.** 2/3	**465.** 5/6
466. 5	**467.** 4/5	**468.** 2 3/4	**469.** 8 6/7	**470.** 7 1/3
471. 5	**472.** 8	**473.** 6 1/15	**474.** 3	**475.** 3
476. 1/6	**477.** 2 2/3	**478.** 9	**479.** 4/5	**480.** 8 3/14

Page 33: Percent

481. 10%	**482.** 347	**483.** 65.6	**484.** 514	**485.** 263
486. 0.25	**487.** 15%	**488.** 73	**489.** 8%	**490.** 97.05
491. 20%	**492.** 25%	**493.** 535	**494.** 927	**495.** 10%
496. 385	**497.** 8.25	**498.** 726	**499.** 13.4	**500.** 32.88

Page 34: Percent

501. 2.4	**502.** 21.5	**503.** 95	**504.** 15%
505. 76	**506.** 26	**507.** 47.2	**508.** 20%
509. 346	**510.** 242.75	**511.** 8%	**512.** 10.54
513. 103.05	**514.** 20%	**515.** 5%	**516.** 63.6
517. 386	**518.** 821	**519.** 800	**520.** 5%

Page 35: Percent

521. 20%	**522.** 15.45	**523.** 5%	**524.** 10.1	**525.** 175
526. 25%	**527.** 613	**528.** 108	**529.** 2.58	**530.** 530
531. 25%	**532.** 8%	**533.** 819	**534.** 736	**535.** 13.05
536. 496	**537.** 110.8	**538.** 353	**539.** 61.52	**540.** 5%

Page 36: Percent

541. 5%	**542.** 2%	**543.** 91.9	**544.** 86	**545.** 101.4
546. 976	**547.** 656	**548.** 2%	**549.** 20%	**550.** 5%

SUMMER MATH SUCCESS

Name: ______ Class: ______

551. 15% 552. 8% 553. 81.3 554. 685 555. 414
556. 15% 557. 6.56 558. 68 559. 337 560. 873

Page 37: Percent

561. 103.8 562. 126 563. 20% 564. 5% 565. 183
566. 67.5 567. 15% 568. 683 569. 20% 570. 12.84
571. 25% 572. 26.4 573. 936 574. 631 575. 10%
576. 5% 577. 10.54 578. 658 579. 17.25 580. 10%

Page 38: Percent and Decimals

581. 0.86 582. 0.38 583. 0.13 584. 0.62 585. 0.48 586. 0.78
587. 0.47 588. 0.79 589. 0.93 590. 0.63 591. 0.14 592. 0.98
593. 0.31 594. 0.1 595. 0.8 596. 0.83 597. 0.24 598. 0.11
599. 0.4 600. 0.16

Page 39: Percent and Decimals

601. 0.22 602. 0.78 603. 0.34 604. 0.61 605. 0.56 606. 0.07
607. 0.21 608. 0.83 609. 0.38 610. 0.72 611. 0.62 612. 0.67
613. 0.82 614. 0.27 615. 0.52 616. 0.6 617. 0.37 618. 0.23
619. 0.88 620. 0.85

Page 40: Percent and Decimals

621. 0.24 622. 0.4 623. 0.43 624. 0.25 625. 0.37 626. 0.77
627. 0.73 628. 0.08 629. 0.89 630. 0.46 631. 0.74 632. 0.47
633. 0.27 634. 1 635. 0.13 636. 0.19 637. 0.23 638. 0.86
639. 0.42 640. 0.32

Page 41: Percent and Decimals

641. 0.61 642. 0.59 643. 0.49 644. 0.29 645. 0.09 646. 0.97

SUMMER MATH SUCCESS

Name: ____________ Class: ________

647. 0.01	**648.** 0.98	**649.** 0.6	**650.** 0.39	**651.** 0.56	**652.** 0.17
653. 0.28	**654.** 0.37	**655.** 0.55	**656.** 0.95	**657.** 0.18	**658.** 0.31
659. 0.71	**660.** 0.45				

Page 42: Percent and Decimals

661. 0.1	**662.** 0.31	**663.** 0.83	**664.** 0.16	**665.** 0.61	**666.** 0.25
667. 0.41	**668.** 0.14	**669.** 0.33	**670.** 0.38	**671.** 0.52	**672.** 0.82
673. 0.57	**674.** 0.65	**675.** 0.91	**676.** 0.15	**677.** 0.17	**678.** 0.4
679. 0.76	**680.** 0.49				

Page 43: Percent and Decimals

681. 51%	**682.** 91%	**683.** 57%	**684.** 19%	**685.** 90%	**686.** 46%
687. 1%	**688.** 92%	**689.** 16%	**690.** 97%	**691.** 22%	**692.** 30%
693. 76%	**694.** 33%	**695.** 69%	**696.** 84%	**697.** 27%	**698.** 5%
699. 35%	**700.** 72%				

Page 44: Percent and Decimals

701. 13%	**702.** 90%	**703.** 4%	**704.** 15%	**705.** 31%	**706.** 70%
707. 35%	**708.** 83%	**709.** 33%	**710.** 26%	**711.** 7%	**712.** 51%
713. 38%	**714.** 96%	**715.** 32%	**716.** 46%	**717.** 37%	**718.** 85%
719. 95%	**720.** 89%				

Page 45: Percent and Decimals

721. 59%	**722.** 46%	**723.** 33%	**724.** 84%	**725.** 57%	**726.** 93%
727. 22%	**728.** 50%	**729.** 87%	**730.** 23%	**731.** 47%	**732.** 78%
733. 56%	**734.** 15%	**735.** 97%	**736.** 77%	**737.** 85%	**738.** 28%
739. 48%	**740.** 44%				

SUMMER MATH SUCCESS

Name: ________ Class: ________

Page 46: Percent and Decimals

741. 7%	**742.** 66%	**743.** 78%	**744.** 6%	**745.** 82%	**746.** 88%
747. 95%	**748.** 56%	**749.** 68%	**750.** 51%	**751.** 38%	**752.** 19%
753. 2%	**754.** 46%	**755.** 58%	**756.** 48%	**757.** 13%	**758.** 43%
759. 61%	**760.** 83%				

Page 47: Percent and Decimals

761. 40%	**762.** 82%	**763.** 60%	**764.** 74%	**765.** 81%	**766.** 36%
767. 69%	**768.** 52%	**769.** 57%	**770.** 48%	**771.** 47%	**772.** 46%
773. 56%	**774.** 78%	**775.** 76%	**776.** 5%	**777.** 27%	**778.** 95%
779. 19%	**780.** 72%				

Page 48: Percent - Advanced

781. 1.168	**782.** 3	**783.** 0.456	**784.** 4.3%	**785.** 39
786. 893	**787.** 0.708	**788.** 0.8%	**789.** 1.18	**790.** 4.7%
791. 0.3%	**792.** 603	**793.** 1.56	**794.** 0.008	**795.** 9.5%
796. 65	**797.** 0.066	**798.** 0.8%	**799.** 4.1%	**800.** 5.8%

Page 49: Percent - Advanced

801. 72	**802.** 4.0%	**803.** 0.9%	**804.** 64
805. 6	**806.** 1.9%	**807.** 0.2%	**808.** 54.717
809. 3	**810.** 9	**811.** 8.6%	**812.** 1
813. 3.5%	**814.** 4.6%	**815.** 7.3%	**816.** 0.35
817. 10.624	**818.** 685	**819.** 518	**820.** 925

Page 50: Percent - Advanced

821. 0.5%	**822.** 2.176	**823.** 4.3%	**824.** 5
825. 0.9%	**826.** 289	**827.** 8	**828.** 8.9%

SUMMER MATH SUCCESS

Name: ________________ Class: __________

829. 8.5%	**830.** 8	**831.** 0.9%	**832.** 2
833. 631	**834.** 7.8%	**835.** 571	**836.** 96
837. 63	**838.** 100	**839.** 71.325	**840.** 0.078

Page 51: Percent - Advanced

841. 6.8%	**842.** 0.759	**843.** 190	**844.** 660
845. 29.82	**846.** 3	**847.** 0.6%	**848.** 5
849. 3	**850.** 10.362	**851.** 0.288	**852.** 0.7%
853. 170	**854.** 9.0%	**855.** 8.3%	**856.** 36
857. 3.8	**858.** 6.1%	**859.** 2.1%	**860.** 0.008

Page 52: Percent - Advanced

861. 42	**862.** 5.917	**863.** 0.1%	**864.** 8	**865.** 2.891
866. 0.3%	**867.** 0.9	**868.** 0.027	**869.** 4.9%	**870.** 0.1%
871. 8.9%	**872.** 0.9%	**873.** 15.39	**874.** 0.2%	**875.** 0.5%
876. 0.6%	**877.** 7.3%	**878.** 7	**879.** 5	**880.** 48

Page 53: Percent - Advanced

881. 422	**882.** 4.71	**883.** 0.9%	**884.** 6.636	**885.** 3
886. 0.396	**887.** 176	**888.** 23	**889.** 62.23	**890.** 96
891. 228	**892.** 7.5%	**893.** 1	**894.** 3	**895.** 27
896. 5.5%	**897.** 4	**898.** 440	**899.** 633	**900.** 0.1%

Page 54: Percent - Advanced

901. 1.83	**902.** 0.6%	**903.** 0.464	**904.** 1.7%	**905.** 0.08
906. 0.6%	**907.** 6.3%	**908.** 55	**909.** 81.42	**910.** 0.3%
911. 4.1%	**912.** 3	**913.** 6.3%	**914.** 22	**915.** 4.8%

SUMMER MATH SUCCESS

Name: ______________ Class: __________

916. 6 917. 9.8% 918. 994 919. 0.6% 920. 418

Page 55: Percent - Advanced

921. 2 922. 969 923. 7.7% 924. 3

925. 5.176 926. 2 927. 1 928. 0.32

929. 0.064 930. 9.0% 931. 0.4% 932. 1

933. 0.9% 934. 72 935. 805 936. 6.5%

937. 5.8% 938. 37.696 939. 6.5% 940. 0.208

Page 56: Percent - Advanced

941. 9.1% 942. 0.3% 943. 7.6% 944. 3.268

945. 0.4% 946. 438 947. 2.2% 948. 7

949. 22.295 950. 5.5% 951. 6 952. 60

953. 0.39 954. 6.1% 955. 3.4% 956. 0.7%

957. 0.2 958. 563 959. 0.018 960. 0.015

Page 57: Percent - Advanced

961. 0.9% 962. 86.112 963. 0.7% 964. 0.1%

965. 0.2% 966. 5 967. 9.3% 968. 2

969. 4.2% 970. 1.413 971. 7.2% 972. 1.96

973. 6.8% 974. 82 975. 0.2% 976. 5

977. 1.584 978. 0.2% 979. 6.8% 980. 5.192

SUMMER MATH SUCCESS

Name: ____________ Class: ________

Page 58: Ratio Conversions

981.

	Ratio	Fraction	Percent	Decimal
a.	1:2	1/2	50%	0.5
b.	3:8	3/8	37.5%	0.375
c.	5:6	5/6	83.3%	0.833
d.	1:6	1/6	16.7%	0.167
e.	1:1	1/1	100%	1
f.	1:5	1/5	20%	0.2
g.	4:7	4/7	57.1%	0.571
h.	1:4	1/4	25%	0.25
i.	5:7	5/7	71.4%	0.714
j.	3:9	3/9	33.3%	0.333
k.	7:10	7/10	70%	0.7
l.	1:8	1/8	12.5%	0.125
m.	3:7	3/7	42.9%	0.429

Page 59: Ratio Conversions

982.

	Ratio	Fraction	Percent	Decimal
a.	8:9	8/9	88.9%	0.889
b.	9:10	9/10	90%	0.9
c.	4:6	4/6	66.7%	0.667
d.	1:8	1/8	12.5%	0.125
e.	1:6	1/6	16.7%	0.167
f.	3:3	3/3	100%	1
g.	1:4	1/4	25%	0.25
h.	3:5	3/5	60%	0.6
i.	6:7	6/7	85.7%	0.857
j.	4:9	4/9	44.4%	0.444
k.	6:9	6/9	66.7%	0.667
l.	2:5	2/5	40%	0.4
m.	4:7	4/7	57.1%	0.571

Page 60: Ratio Conversions

983.

	Ratio	Fraction	Percent	Decimal
a.	1:1	1/1	100%	1
b.	1:2	1/2	50%	0.5
c.	8:10	8/10	80%	0.8
d.	4:8	4/8	50%	0.5
e.	2:8	2/8	25%	0.25
f.	1:4	1/4	25%	0.25
g.	4:6	4/6	66.7%	0.667
h.	5:8	5/8	62.5%	0.625
i.	2:3	2/3	66.7%	0.667
j.	4:10	4/10	40%	0.4
k.	3:7	3/7	42.9%	0.429
l.	7:10	7/10	70%	0.7
m.	5:9	5/9	55.6%	0.556

Page 61: Ratio Conversions

984.

	Ratio	Fraction	Percent	Decimal
a.	2:4	2/4	50%	0.5
b.	2:10	2/10	20%	0.2
c.	3:4	3/4	75%	0.75
d.	3:5	3/5	60%	0.6
e.	5:8	5/8	62.5%	0.625
f.	2:2	2/2	100%	1
g.	2:3	2/3	66.7%	0.667
h.	1:7	1/7	14.3%	0.143
i.	6:10	6/10	60%	0.6
j.	1:3	1/3	33.3%	0.333
k.	7:9	7/9	77.8%	0.778
l.	2:5	2/5	40%	0.4
m.	4:9	4/9	44.4%	0.444

SUMMER MATH SUCCESS

Name: ____________ Class: ________

Page 62: Ratio Conversions

985.

	Ratio	Fraction	Percent	Decimal
a.	7:10	7/10	70%	0.7
b.	3:5	3/5	60%	0.6
c.	1:3	1/3	33.3%	0.333
d.	8:9	8/9	88.9%	0.889
e.	4:10	4/10	40%	0.4
f.	2:5	2/5	40%	0.4
g.	4:5	4/5	80%	0.8
h.	3:10	3/10	30%	0.3
i.	5:6	5/6	83.3%	0.833
j.	1:1	1/1	100%	1
k.	5:8	5/8	62.5%	0.625
l.	2:3	2/3	66.7%	0.667
m.	4:9	4/9	44.4%	0.444

Page 63: Ratio Conversions

986.

	Ratio	Fraction	Percent	Decimal
a.	1:2	1/2	50%	0.5
b.	6:9	6/9	66.7%	0.667
c.	6:7	6/7	85.7%	0.857
d.	2:4	2/4	50%	0.5
e.	1:1	1/1	100%	1
f.	3:5	3/5	60%	0.6
g.	6:8	6/8	75%	0.75
h.	1:6	1/6	16.7%	0.167
i.	2:3	2/3	66.7%	0.667
j.	2:6	2/6	33.3%	0.333
k.	4:8	4/8	50%	0.5
l.	1:4	1/4	25%	0.25
m.	3:4	3/4	75%	0.75

Page 64: Ratio Conversions

987.

	Ratio	Fraction	Percent	Decimal
a.	4:4	4/4	100%	1
b.	1:2	1/2	50%	0.5
c.	2:7	2/7	28.6%	0.286
d.	3:10	3/10	30%	0.3
e.	3:4	3/4	75%	0.75
f.	4:7	4/7	57.1%	0.571
g.	2:8	2/8	25%	0.25
h.	1:4	1/4	25%	0.25
i.	1:5	1/5	20%	0.2
j.	2:5	2/5	40%	0.4
k.	1:3	1/3	33.3%	0.333
l.	4:5	4/5	80%	0.8
m.	3:6	3/6	50%	0.5

SUMMER MATH SUCCESS

Name: ____________ Class: ________

Page 65: Cartesian Coordinates

988.

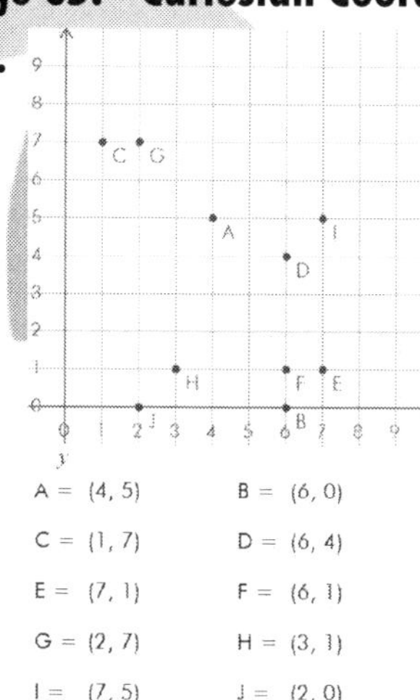

A = (4, 5)	B = (6, 0)
C = (1, 7)	D = (6, 4)
E = (7, 1)	F = (6, 1)
G = (2, 7)	H = (3, 1)
I = (7, 5)	J = (2, 0)

Page 66: Cartesian Coordinates

989.

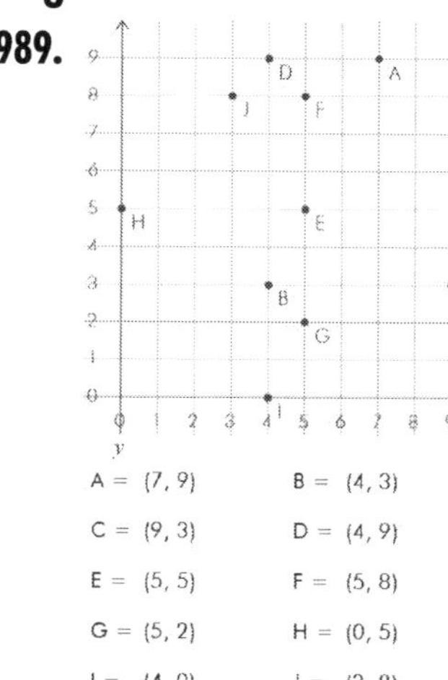

A = (7, 9)	B = (4, 3)
C = (9, 3)	D = (4, 9)
E = (5, 5)	F = (5, 8)
G = (5, 2)	H = (0, 5)
I = (4, 0)	J = (3, 8)

Page 67: Cartesian Coordinates

990.

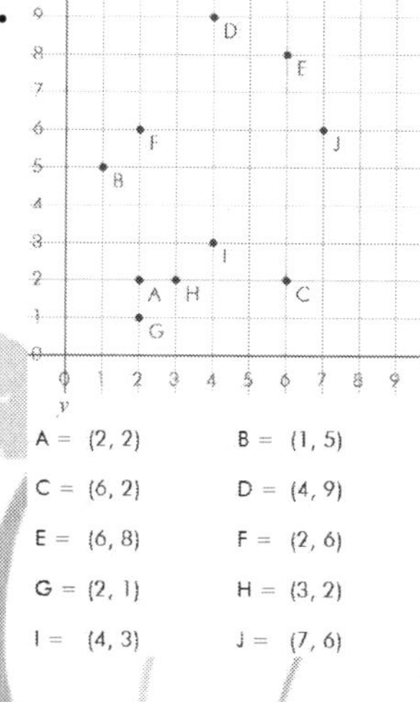

A = (2, 2)	B = (1, 5)
C = (6, 2)	D = (4, 9)
E = (6, 8)	F = (2, 6)
G = (2, 1)	H = (3, 2)
I = (4, 3)	J = (7, 6)

SUMMER MATH SUCCESS

Name: ____________ Class: ________

Page 68: Cartesian Coordinates

991.

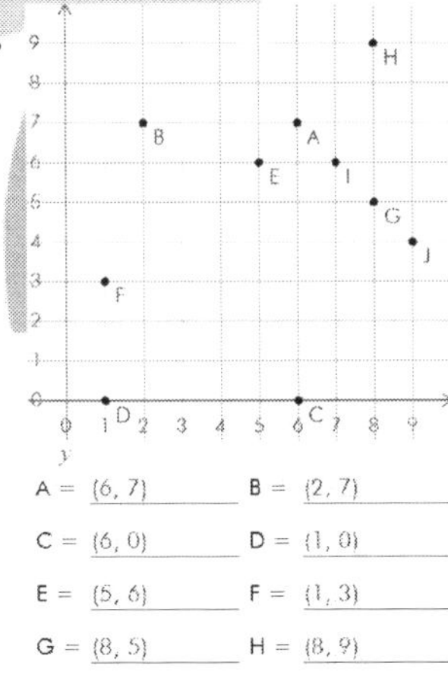

A = (6, 7) B = (2, 7)

C = (6, 0) D = (1, 0)

E = (5, 6) F = (1, 3)

G = (8, 5) H = (8, 9)

I = (7, 6) J = (9, 4)

Page 69: Cartesian Coordinates

992.

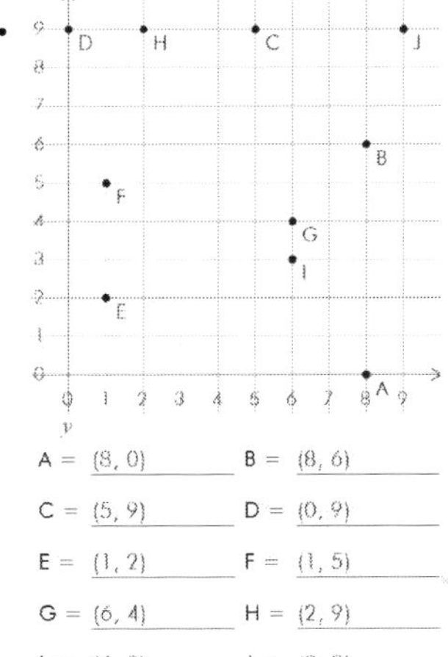

A = (8, 0) B = (8, 6)

C = (5, 9) D = (0, 9)

E = (1, 2) F = (1, 5)

G = (6, 4) H = (2, 9)

I = (6, 3) J = (9, 9)

Page 70: Cartesian Coordinates

993.

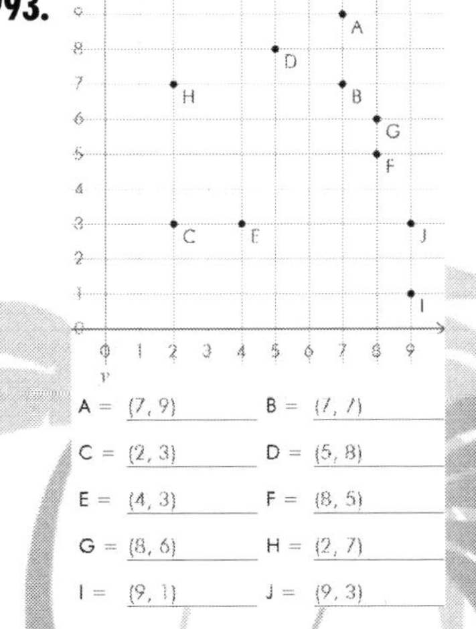

A = (7, 9) B = (7, 7)

C = (2, 3) D = (5, 8)

E = (4, 3) F = (8, 5)

G = (8, 6) H = (2, 7)

I = (9, 1) J = (9, 3)

SUMMER MATH SUCCESS

Name: ____________ Class: ________

Page 71: Cartesian Coordinates With Four Quadrants

994.

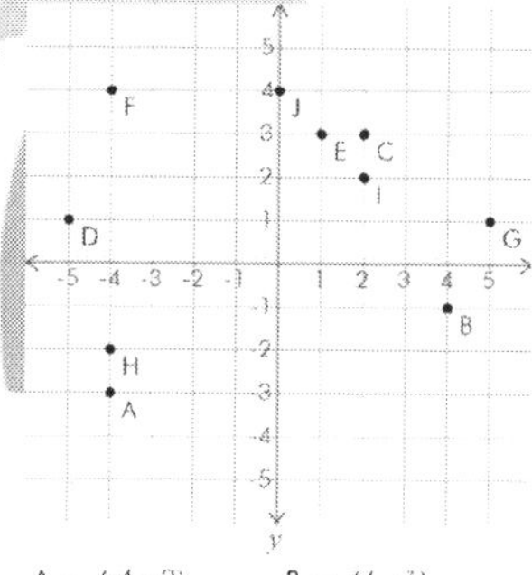

A = (-4, -3) B = (4, -1)

C = (2, 3) D = (-5, 1)

E = (1, 3) F = (-4, 4)

G = (5, 1) H = (-4, -2)

I = (2, 2) J = (0, 4)

Page 72: Cartesian Coordinates With Four Quadrants

995.

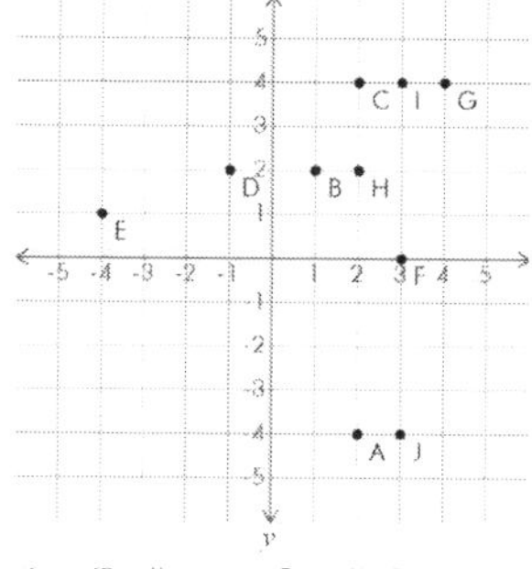

A = (2, -4) B = (1, 2)

C = (2, 4) D = (-1, 2)

E = (-4, 1) F = (3, 0)

G = (4, 4) H = (2, 2)

I = (3, 4) J = (3, -4)

SUMMER MATH SUCCESS

Name: ________________ Class: __________

Page 73: Cartesian Coordinates With Four Quadrants

996.

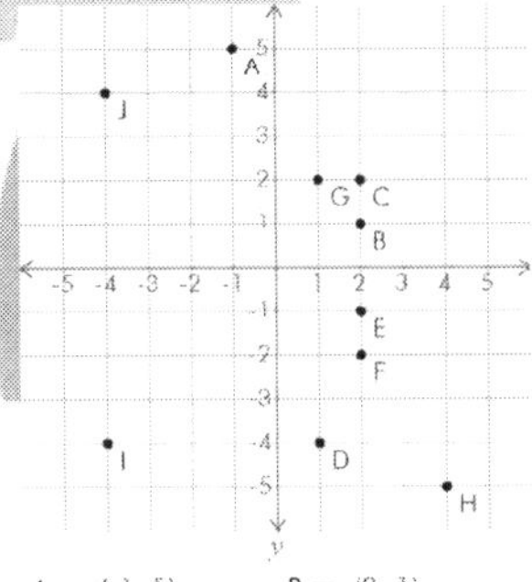

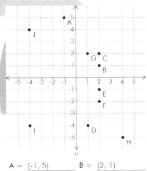

A = (-1, 5) B = (2, 1)

C = (2, 2) D = (1, -4)

E = (2, -1) F = (2, -2)

G = (1, 2) H = (4, -5)

I = (-4, -4) J = (-4, 4)

Page 74: Cartesian Coordinates With Four Quadrants

997.

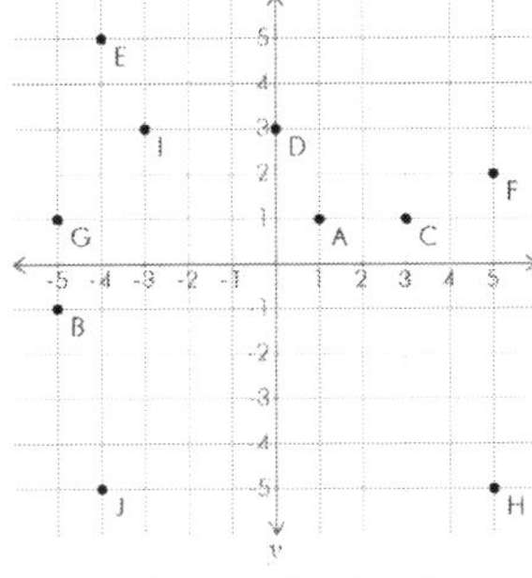

A = (1, 1) B = (-5, -1)

C = (3, 1) D = (0, 3)

E = (-4, 5) F = (5, 2)

G = (-5, 1) H = (5, -5)

I = (-3, 3) J = (-4, -5)

SUMMER MATH SUCCESS

Name: ____________ Class: ________

Page 75: Cartesian Coordinates With Four Quadrants

998.

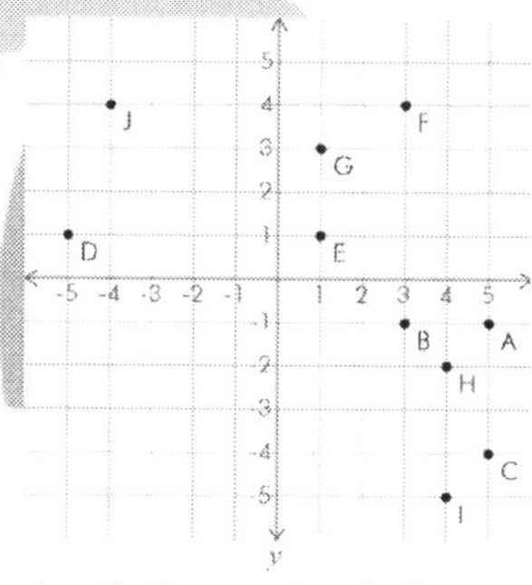

A = (5, -1) B = (3, -1)

C = (5, -4) D = (-5, 1)

E = (1, 1) F = (3, 4)

G = (1, 3) H = (4, -2)

I = (4, -5) J = (-4, 4)

Page 76: Cartesian Coordinates With Four Quadrants

999.

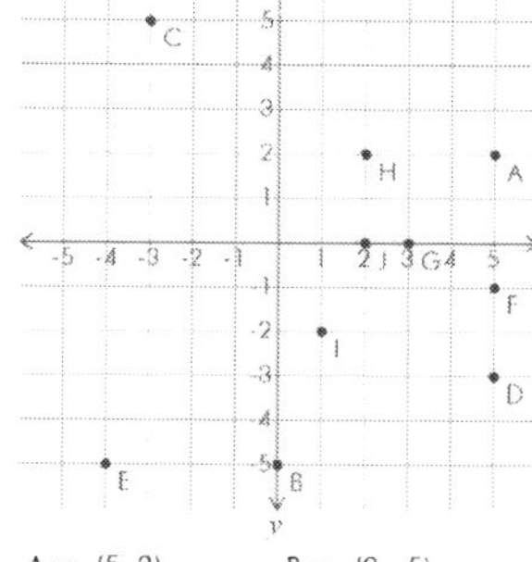

A = (5, 2) B = (0, -5)

C = (-3, 5) D = (5, -3)

E = (-4, -5) F = (5, -1)

G = (3, 0) H = (2, 2)

I = (1, -2) J = (2, 0)

SUMMER MATH SUCCESS

Name: ______________ Class: __________

Page 77: Cartesian Coordinates With Four Quadrants

1000.

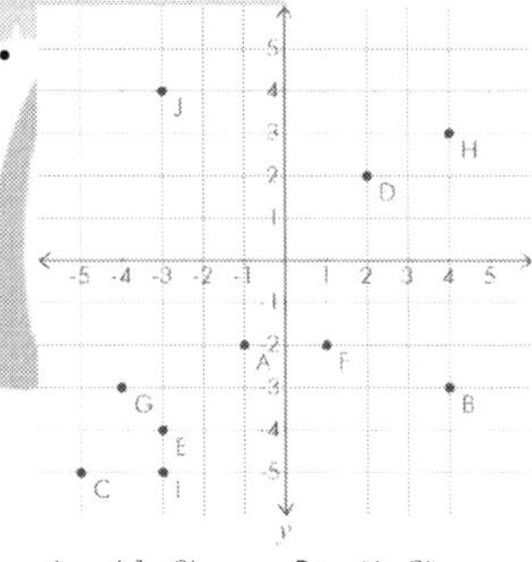

A = (-1, -2) B = (4, -3)

C = (-5, -5) D = (2, 2)

E = (-3, -4) F = (1, -2)

G = (-4, -3) H = (4, 3)

I = (-3, -5) J = (-3, 4)

Page 78: Cartesian Coordinates With Four Quadrants

1001.

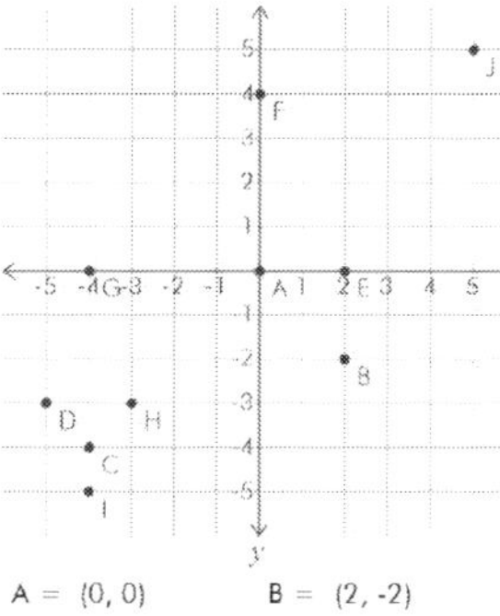

A = (0, 0) B = (2, -2)

C = (-4, -4) D = (-5, -3)

E = (2, 0) F = (0, 4)

G = (-4, 0) H = (-3, -3)

I = (-4, -5) J = (5, 5)

SUMMER MATH SUCCESS

Name: ________________ Class: __________

Page 79: Cartesian Coordinates With Four Quadrants

1002.

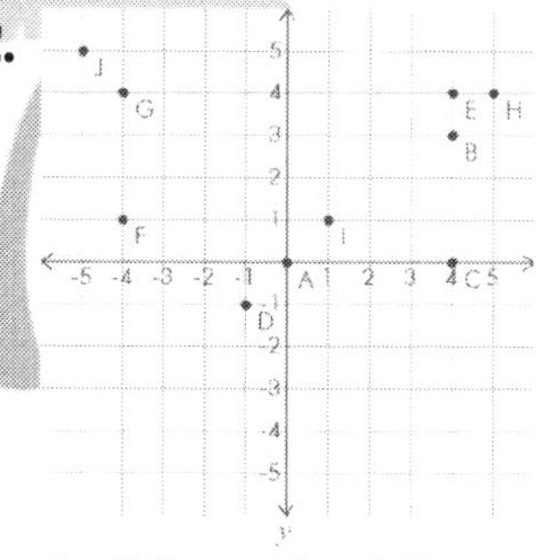

A = (0, 0) B = (4, 3)

C = (4, 0) D = (-1, -1)

E = (4, 4) F = (-4, 1)

G = (-4, 4) H = (5, 4)

I = (1, 1) J = (-5, 5)

Page 80: Cartesian Coordinates With Four Quadrants

1003.

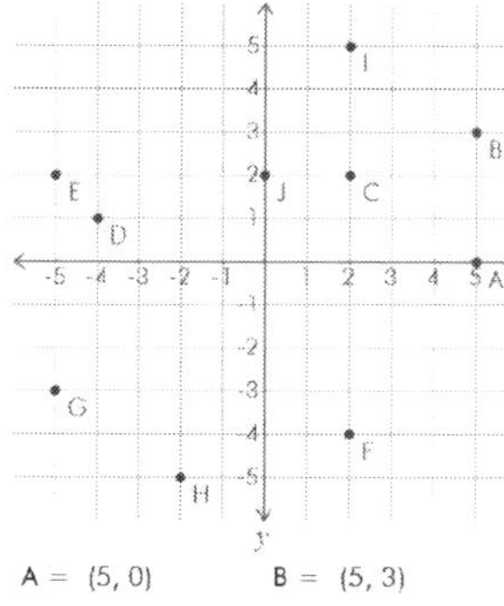

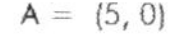

A = (5, 0) B = (5, 3)

C = (2, 2) D = (-4, 1)

E = (-5, 2) F = (2, -4)

G = (-5, -3) H = (-2, -5)

I = (2, 5) J = (0, 2)

Page 81: Plot Lines

1004.

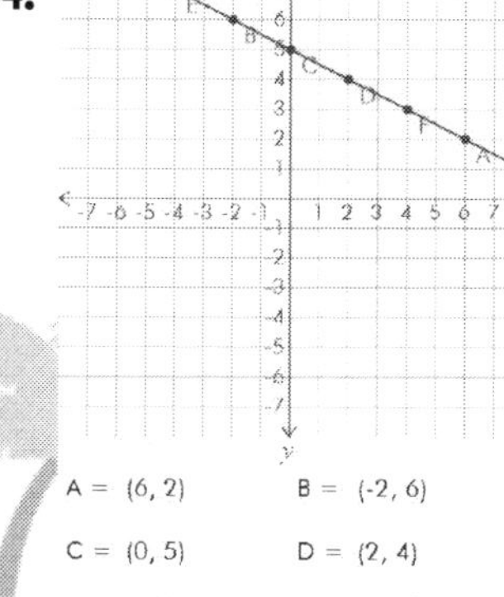

A = (6, 2) B = (-2, 6)

C = (0, 5) D = (2, 4)

E = (-4, 7) F = (4, 3)

SUMMER MATH SUCCESS

Name: ____________ Class: ________

Page 82: Plot Lines

1005.

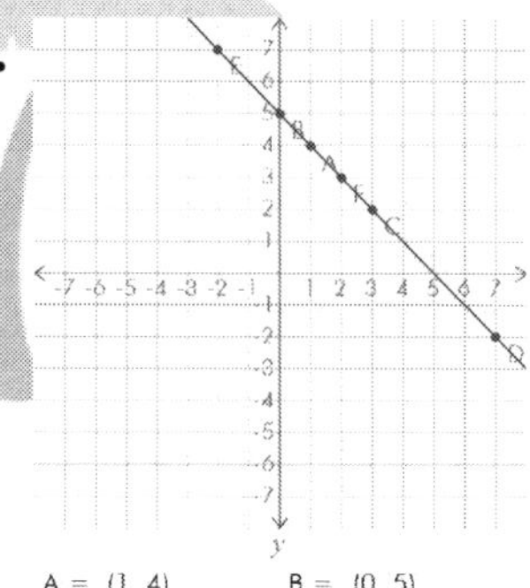

A = (1, 4) B = (0, 5)

C = (3, 2) D = (7, -2)

E = (-2, 7) F = (2, 3)

Page 83: Plot Lines

1006.

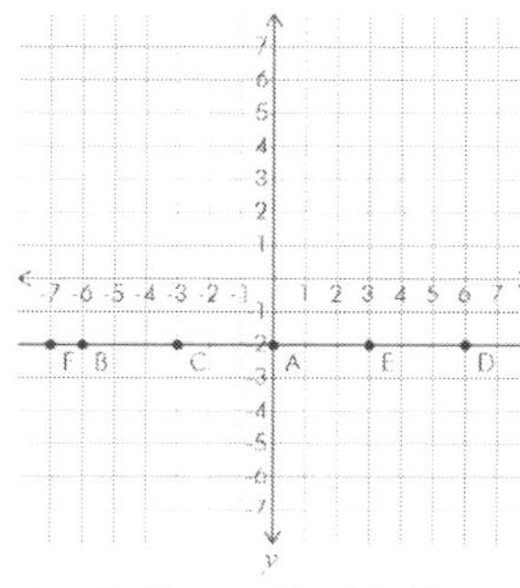

A = (0, -2) B = (-6, -2)

C = (-3, -2) D = (6, -2)

E = (3, -2) F = (-7, -2)

Page 84: Plot Lines

1007.

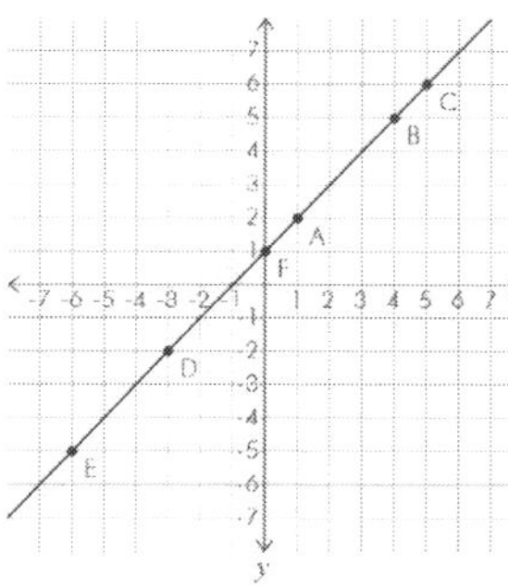

A = (1, 2) B = (4, 5)

C = (5, 6) D = (-3, -2)

E = (-6, -5) F = (0, 1)

SUMMER MATH SUCCESS

Name: ____________________ Class: __________

Page 85: Plot Lines

1008.

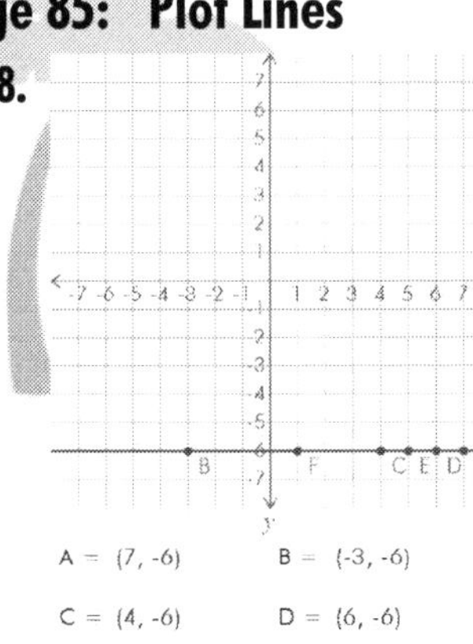

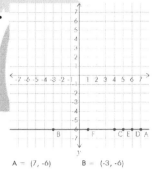

A = (7, -6) B = (-3, -6)

C = (4, -6) D = (6, -6)

E = (5, -6) F = (1, -6)

Page 86: Plot Lines

1009.

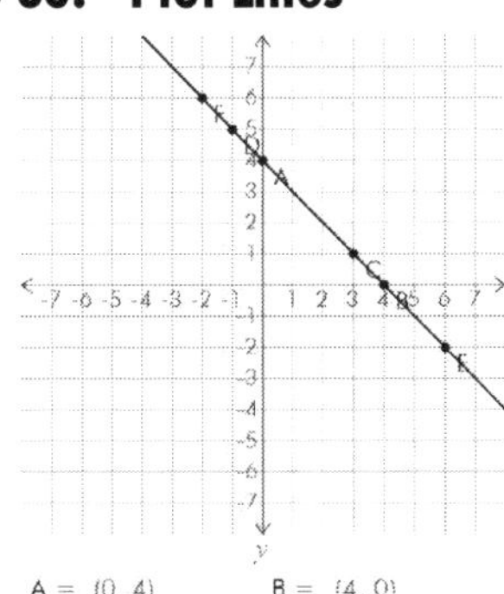

A = (0, 4) B = (4, 0)

C = (3, 1) D = (-1, 5)

E = (6, -2) F = (-2, 6)

Page 87: Plot Lines

1010.

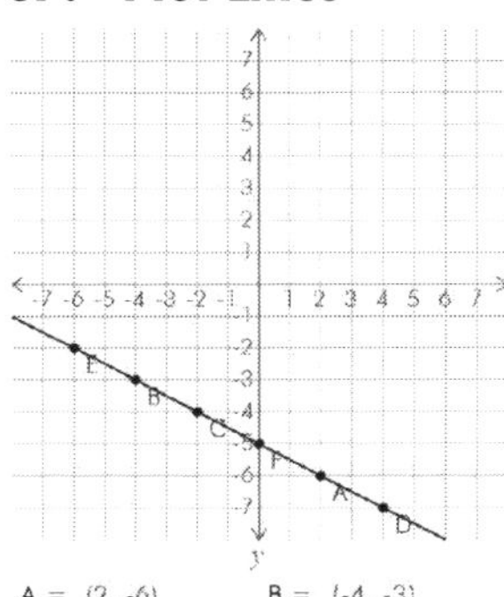

A = (2, -6) B = (-4, -3)

C = (-2, -4) D = (4, -7)

E = (-6, -2) F = (0, -5)

SUMMER MATH SUCCESS

Name: ______________ Class: __________

Page 88: Plot Lines

1011.

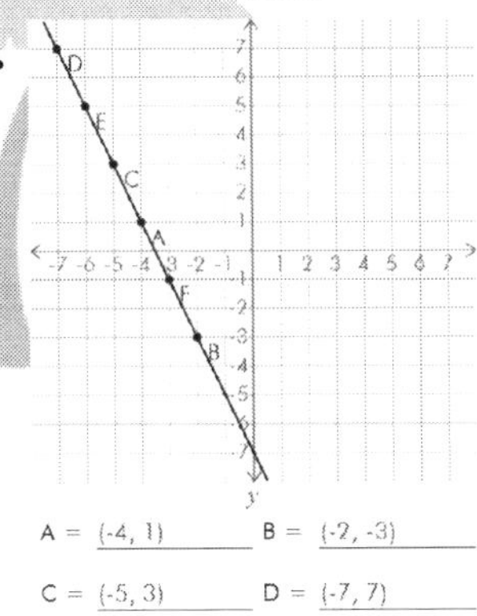

A = (-4, 1) B = (-2, -3)

C = (-5, 3) D = (-7, 7)

E = (-6, 5) F = (-3, -1)

Page 89: Plot Lines

1012.

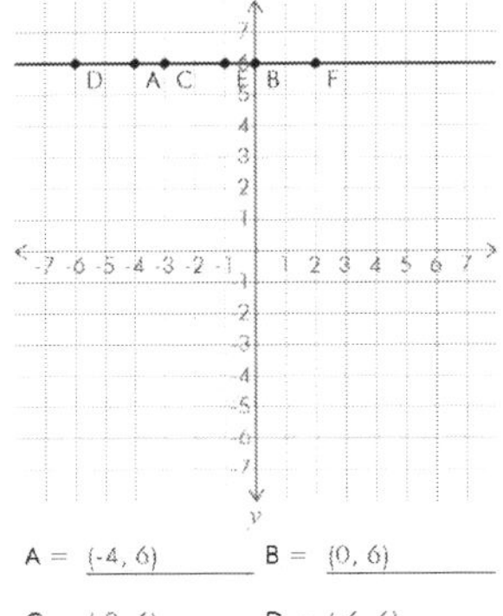

A = (-4, 6) B = (0, 6)

C = (-3, 6) D = (-6, 6)

E = (-1, 6) F = (2, 6)

Page 90: Plot Lines

1013.

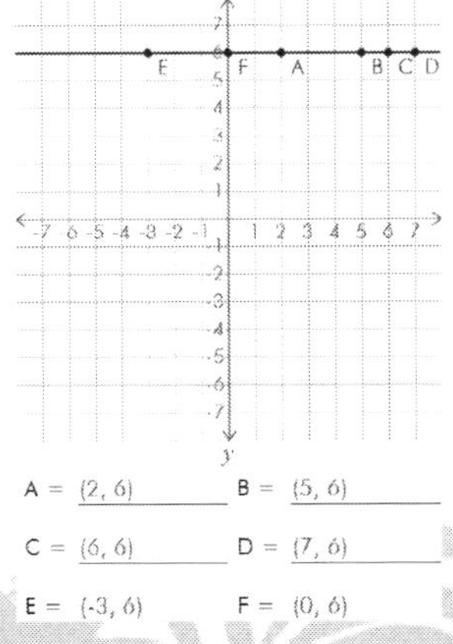

A = (2, 6) B = (5, 6)

C = (6, 6) D = (7, 6)

E = (-3, 6) F = (0, 6)

Page 91: Exponents

1014. 36 **1015.** 50,653 **1016.** 81 **1017.** 441

1018. 8,000 **1019.** 3,249 **1020.** 32,768 **1021.** 49

Name: ____________ Class: ________

1022. 1,225 1023. 529 1024. 5,041 1025. 421,875
1026. 1,331 1027. 571,787 1028. 4,096 1029. 21,952
1030. 1,369 1031. 4,624 1032. 1,600 1033. 2,197

Page 92: Exponents

1034. 16 1035. 195,112 1036. 625 1037. 314,432
1038. 54,872 1039. 4,356 1040. 529 1041. 2,704
1042. 5,041 1043. 35,937 1044. 1,156 1045. 274,625
1046. 6,859 1047. 1 1048. 166,375 1049. 205,379
1050. 1,225 1051. 59,319 1052. 3,721 1053. 125,000

Page 93: Exponents

1054. 64 1055. 625 1056. 841 1057. 148,877
1058. 238,328 1059. 3,375 1060. 389,017 1061. 125,000
1062. 2,744 1063. 2,197 1064. 970,299 1065. 6,561
1066. 2,025 1067. 5,041 1068. 484 1069. 35,937
1070. 205,379 1071. 5,776 1072. 7,396 1073. 64,000

Page 94: Exponents

1074. 4,225 1075. 4,356 1076. 195,112 1077. 21,952
1078. 5,476 1079. 2,025 1080. 512 1081. 169
1082. 144 1083. 729 1084. 1,296 1085. 7,056
1086. 7,744 1087. 324 1088. 592,704 1089. 49
1090. 1 1091. 529 1092. 4,624 1093. 16

Page 95: Exponents

1094. 3,025 1095. 12,167 1096. 6,241 1097. 79,507

SUMMER MATH SUCCESS

Name: ____________ Class: ________

1098. 27,000
1099. 729,000
1100. 10,648
1101. 100
1102. 2,304
1103. 196
1104. 4,096
1105. 484
1106. 9,801
1107. 405,224
1108. 140,608
1109. 441
1110. 148,877
1111. 6,724
1112. 117,649
1113. 2,500

Page 96: Scientific Notation

1114. 4.92 × 10^5
1115. 3.346 × 10^6
1116. 1.486 × 10^6
1117. 7.162 × 10^6
1118. 7.6 × 10^6
1119. 6.64 × 10^5
1120. 1.249 × 10^6
1121. 9.25 × 10^6
1122. 9.8 × 10^6
1123. 8.12 × 10^6
1124. 3.2 × 10^6
1125. 6.78 × 10^6
1126. 8.2 × 10^6
1127. 3.589 × 10^6
1128. 7.4 × 10^6
1129. 9.89 × 10^6
1130. 3.49 × 10^6
1131. 5.02 × 10^6
1132. 4.53 × 10^6
1133. 1.543 × 10^6

Page 97: Scientific Notation

1134. 5 × 10^6
1135. 7.088 × 10^6
1136. 5.76 × 10^6
1137. 8.674 × 10^6
1138. 5.925 × 10^6
1139. 1.2 × 10^5
1140. 1.795 × 10^6
1141. 5.6 × 10^4
1142. 2.3 × 10^5
1143. 5.4 × 10^6
1144. 2.03 × 10^6
1145. 1.52 × 10^6
1146. 4.94 × 10^6
1147. 2.52 × 10^6

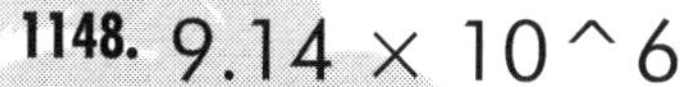

Name: ________________ Class: __________

1148. 9.14 × 10^6

1149. 6.49 × 10^5

1150. 9.9 × 10^6

1151. 4.385 × 10^6

1152. 8.92 × 10^6

1153. 1.86 × 10^6

Page 98: Scientific Notation

1154. 1.169 × 10^6

1155. 6.067 × 10^6

1156. 5.46 × 10^6

1157. 3.03 × 10^6

1158. 5.37 × 10^6

1159. 5.5 × 10^6

1160. 4.52 × 10^6

1161. 9.4 × 10^6

1162. 8.4 × 10^6

1163. 8.8 × 10^6

1164. 7.3 × 10^6

1165. 9.2 × 10^6

1166. 2.4 × 10^6

1167. 1.9 × 10^4

1168. 4.6 × 10^6

1169. 9.74 × 10^6

1170. 9 × 10^6

1171. 5.4 × 10^5

1172. 9.6 × 10^6

1173. 3.38 × 10^6

Page 99: Scientific Notation

1174. 8,400,000

1175. 8,500,000

1176. 3,620,000

1177. 2,300,000

1178. 8,437,000

1179. 5,668,000

1180. 6,343,000

1181. 9,780,000

1182. 4,270,000

1183. 3,500,000

1184. 1,300,000

1185. 6,123,000

1186. 1,500,000

1187. 6,040,000

1188. 9,930,000

1189. 1,075,000

1190. 8,800,000

1191. 3,640,000

1192. 2,400,000

1193. 8,330,000

SUMMER MATH SUCCESS

Name: ________________ Class: __________

Page 100: Scientific Notation

1194. 7,700,000 1195. 4,700,000 1196. 65,000
1197. 5,392,000 1198. 3,190,000 1199. 492,000
1200. 7,800,000 1201. 5,140,000 1202. 7,150,000
1203. 8,500,000 1204. 8,940,000 1205. 3,960,000
1206. 7,161,000 1207. 743,000 1208. 5,420,000
1209. 2,600,000 1210. 5,162,000 1211. 5,200,000
1212. 7,390,000 1213. 9,700,000

Page 101: Scientific Notation

1214. 7,400,000 1215. 3,270,000 1216. 3,140,000
1217. 9,547,000 1218. 5,695,000 1219. 8,840,000
1220. 3,893,000 1221. 6,000,000 1222. 6,759,000
1223. 4,300,000 1224. 8,726,000 1225. 4,398,000
1226. 2,725,000 1227. 942,000 1228. 5,110,000
1229. 8,800,000 1230. 8,920,000 1231. 3,400,000
1232. 2,560,000 1233. 1,600,000

Page 102: Expressions - Single Step

1234. 2 1235. 5 1236. 5 1237. 8 1238. 7 1239. 7 1240. 4 1241. 9
1242. 4 1243. 1 1244. 8 1245. 9 1246. 4 1247. 2 1248. 3 1249. 3
1250. 4 1251. 5 1252. 3 1253. 7

Page 103: Expressions - Single Step

1254. 6 1255. 3 1256. 8 1257. 7 1258. 1 1259. 3 1260. 7 1261. 8
1262. 8 1263. 5 1264. 7 1265. 4 1266. 1 1267. 5 1268. 7 1269. 5

SUMMER
MATH SUCCESS

Name: ________________ Class: __________

1270. 9 1271. 3 1272. 5 1273. 4

Page 104: Expressions - Single Step

1274. 1 1275. 9 1276. 8 1277. 2 1278. 9 1279. 4 1280. 9 1281. 2

1282. 5 1283. 5 1284. 3 1285. 4 1286. 2 1287. 1 1288. 3 1289. 7

1290. 5 1291. 5 1292. 1 1293. 6

Page 105: Expressions - Single Step

1294. 6 1295. 1 1296. 7 1297. 5 1298. 5 1299. 6 1300. 7 1301. 1

1302. 7 1303. 7 1304. 8 1305. 3 1306. 1 1307. 4 1308. 7 1309. 2

1310. 6 1311. 5 1312. 9 1313. 7

Page 106: Expressions - Single Step

1314. 7 1315. 5 1316. 4 1317. 9 1318. 5 1319. 2 1320. 1 1321. 1

1322. 9 1323. 1 1324. 6 1325. 8 1326. 1 1327. 4 1328. 5 1329. 1

1330. 1 1331. 8 1332. 1 1333. 2

Page 107: Number Problems

1334. 3 1335. 51 1336. 25 1337. 22 1338. 20 1339. 17 1340. 26

1341. 27 1342. 30 1343. 20

Page 108: Number Problems

1344. 14 1345. 19 1346. 20 1347. 6 1348. 18 1349. 15 1350. 29

1351. 17 1352. 21 1353. 17

Page 109: Number Problems

1354. 14 1355. 22 1356. 19 1357. 15 1358. 14 1359. 10 1360. 6

1361. 36 1362. 26 1363. 14

Page 110: Pre-Algebra Equations (One Step) Addition and Subtraction

1364. $x = 2$ 1365. $x = 6$ 1366. $x = 7$ 1367. $x = 7$ 1368. $x = 7$

SUMMER MATH SUCCESS

Name: ________________ Class: __________

1369. x = 4 1370. x = 3 1371. x = 2 1372. x = 3 1373. x = 6

1374. x = 4 1375. x = 7 1376. x = 9 1377. x = 8 1378. x = 6

1379. x = 8 1380. x = 8 1381. x = 2 1382. x = 7 1383. x = 6

Page 111: Pre-Algebra Equations (One Step) Addition and Subtraction

1384. x = 3 1385. x = 3 1386. x = 8 1387. x = 4 1388. x = 9

1389. x = 6 1390. x = 5 1391. x = 1 1392. x = 4 1393. x = 8

1394. x = 4 1395. x = 9 1396. x = 5 1397. x = 5 1398. x = 1

1399. x = 8 1400. x = 1 1401. x = 3 1402. x = 7 1403. x = 9

Page 112: Pre-Algebra Equations (One Step) Addition and Subtraction

1404. x = 2 1405. x = 4 1406. x = 6 1407. x = 3 1408. x = 8

1409. x = 5 1410. x = 6 1411. x = 8 1412. x = 7 1413. x = 5

1414. x = 9 1415. x = 2 1416. x = 1 1417. x = 7 1418. x = 1

1419. x = 7 1420. x = 6 1421. x = 9 1422. x = 1 1423. x = 5

Page 113: Pre-Algebra Equations (One Step) Addition and Subtraction

1424. x = 1 1425. x = 7 1426. x = 8 1427. x = 5 1428. x = 5

1429. x = 9 1430. x = 5 1431. x = 4 1432. x = 4 1433. x = 2

1434. x = 7 1435. x = 9 1436. x = 7 1437. x = 6 1438. x = 7

1439. x = 9 1440. x = 4 1441. x = 1 1442. x = 5 1443. x = 8

Page 114: Pre-Algebra Equations (One Step) Addition and Subtraction

1444. x = 4 1445. x = 2 1446. x = 3 1447. x = 8 1448. x = 7

1449. x = 4 1450. x = 8 1451. x = 7 1452. x = 1 1453. x = 1

1454. x = 6 1455. x = 4 1456. x = 2 1457. x = 1 1458. x = 7

1459. x = 9 1460. x = 1 1461. x = 5 1462. x = 9 1463. x = 7

SUMMER MATH SUCCESS

Name: ____________ Class: ________

Page 115: Pre-Algebra Equations (One Step) Addition and Subtraction

1464. $x = 4$ 1465. $x = 4$ 1466. $x = 2$ 1467. $x = 6$ 1468. $x = 1$
1469. $x = 6$ 1470. $x = 5$ 1471. $x = 9$ 1472. $x = 2$ 1473. $x = 8$
1474. $x = 5$ 1475. $x = 8$ 1476. $x = 4$ 1477. $x = 5$ 1478. $x = 5$
1479. $x = 1$ 1480. $x = 5$ 1481. $x = 9$ 1482. $x = 9$ 1483. $x = 7$

Page 116: Pre-Algebra Equations (One Step) Addition and Subtraction

1484. $x = 6$ 1485. $x = 7$ 1486. $x = 7$ 1487. $x = 6$ 1488. $x = 2$
1489. $x = 1$ 1490. $x = 7$ 1491. $x = 3$ 1492. $x = 5$ 1493. $x = 9$
1494. $x = 7$ 1495. $x = 4$ 1496. $x = 1$ 1497. $x = 5$ 1498. $x = 2$
1499. $x = 8$ 1500. $x = 4$ 1501. $x = 7$ 1502. $x = 3$ 1503. $x = 7$

Page 117: Pre-Algebra Equations (One Step) Addition and Subtraction

1504. $x = 9$ 1505. $x = 5$ 1506. $x = 6$ 1507. $x = 3$ 1508. $x = 5$
1509. $x = 7$ 1510. $x = 5$ 1511. $x = 8$ 1512. $x = 6$ 1513. $x = 8$
1514. $x = 7$ 1515. $x = 3$ 1516. $x = 9$ 1517. $x = 9$ 1518. $x = 9$
1519. $x = 2$ 1520. $x = 6$ 1521. $x = 3$ 1522. $x = 2$ 1523. $x = 1$

Page 118: Pre-Algebra Equations (One Step) Addition and Subtraction

1524. $x = 5$ 1525. $x = 7$ 1526. $x = 9$ 1527. $x = 3$ 1528. $x = 8$
1529. $x = 7$ 1530. $x = 7$ 1531. $x = 6$ 1532. $x = 8$ 1533. $x = 1$
1534. $x = 2$ 1535. $x = 6$ 1536. $x = 7$ 1537. $x = 6$ 1538. $x = 7$
1539. $x = 7$ 1540. $x = 5$ 1541. $x = 2$ 1542. $x = 8$ 1543. $x = 9$

Page 119: Pre-Algebra Equations (One Step) Addition and Subtraction

1544. $x = 9$ 1545. $x = 1$ 1546. $x = 8$ 1547. $x = 6$ 1548. $x = 1$
1549. $x = 4$ 1550. $x = 4$ 1551. $x = 6$ 1552. $x = 6$ 1553. $x = 5$
1554. $x = 5$ 1555. $x = 2$ 1556. $x = 1$ 1557. $x = 8$ 1558. $x = 9$

SUMMER MATH SUCCESS

Name: ____________ Class: ________

1559. x = 6 1560. x = 2 1561. x = 8 1562. x = 6 1563. x = 9

Page 120: Pre-Algebra Equations (One Step) Multiplication and Division

1564. x = 7 1565. x = 9 1566. x = 10 1567. x = 4

1568. x = 4 1569. x = 5 1570. x = 9 1571. x = 7

1572. x = 3 1573. x = 2 1574. x = 1 1575. x = 6

1576. x = 8 1577. x = 6 1578. x = 6 1579. x = 5

1580. x = 5 1581. x = 8 1582. x = 1 1583. x = 7

Page 121: Pre-Algebra Equations (One Step) Multiplication and Division

1584. x = 2 1585. x = 2 1586. x = 1 1587. x = 4 1588. x = 7

1589. x = 5 1590. x = 1 1591. x = 5 1592. x = 7 1593. x = 8

1594. x = 9 1595. x = 8 1596. x = 3 1597. x = 8 1598. x = 4

1599. x = 3 1600. x = 9 1601. x = 7 1602. x = 1 1603. x = 6

Page 122: Pre-Algebra Equations (One Step) Multiplication and Division

1604. x = 3 1605. x = 6 1606. x = 28 1607. x = 6

1608. x = 3 1609. x = 16 1610. x = 5 1611. x = 6

1612. x = 2 1613. x = 3 1614. x = 2 1615. x = 8

1616. x = 6 1617. x = 3 1618. x = 3 1619. x = 63

1620. x = 1 1621. x = 1 1622. x = 6 1623. x = 9

Page 123: Pre-Algebra Equations (One Step) Multiplication and Division

1624. x = 4 1625. x = 5 1626. x = 9 1627. x = 9

1628. x = 2 1629. x = 6 1630. x = 1 1631. x = 3

1632. x = 1 1633. x = 24 1634. x = 8 1635. x = 8

1636. x = 5 1637. x = 6 1638. x = 1 1639. x = 5

SUMMER MATH SUCCESS

Name: ____________ Class: ________

1640. $x = 3$ 1641. $x = 12$ 1642. $x = 7$ 1643. $x = 4$

Page 124: Pre-Algebra Equations (One Step) Multiplication and Division

1644. $x = 2$ 1645. $x = 5$ 1646. $x = 7$ 1647. $x = 2$

1648. $x = 1$ 1649. $x = 5$ 1650. $x = 3$ 1651. $x = 4$

1652. $x = 6$ 1653. $x = 8$ 1654. $x = 1$ 1655. $x = 9$

1656. $x = 40$ 1657. $x = 7$ 1658. $x = 5$ 1659. $x = 9$

1660. $x = 16$ 1661. $x = 24$ 1662. $x = 5$ 1663. $x = 8$

Page 125: Pre-Algebra Equations (One Step) Multiplication and Division

1664. $x = 8$ 1665. $x = 5$ 1666. $x = 3$ 1667. $x = 3$

1668. $x = 4$ 1669. $x = 54$ 1670. $x = 6$ 1671. $x = 7$

1672. $x = 6$ 1673. $x = 5$ 1674. $x = 24$ 1675. $x = 3$

1676. $x = 5$ 1677. $x = 20$ 1678. $x = 2$ 1679. $x = 2$

1680. $x = 1$ 1681. $x = 4$ 1682. $x = 9$ 1683. $x = 2$

Page 126: Pre-Algebra Equations (One Step) Multiplication and Division

1684. $x = 7$ 1685. $x = 4$ 1686. $x = 7$ 1687. $x = 2$

1688. $x = 8$ 1689. $x = 7$ 1690. $x = 7$ 1691. $x = 9$

1692. $x = 2$ 1693. $x = 2$ 1694. $x = 6$ 1695. $x = 4$

1696. $x = 5$ 1697. $x = 2$ 1698. $x = 18$ 1699. $x = 7$

1700. $x = 72$ 1701. $x = 9$ 1702. $x = 3$ 1703. $x = 6$

Page 127: Pre-Algebra Equations (One Step) Multiplication and Division

1704. $x = 5$ 1705. $x = 8$ 1706. $x = 54$ 1707. $x = 9$

1708. $x = 6$ 1709. $x = 4$ 1710. $x = 4$ 1711. $x = 5$

1712. $x = 30$ 1713. $x = 1$ 1714. $x = 9$ 1715. $x = 2$

SUMMER MATH SUCCESS

Name: ________________ Class: __________

1716. $x = 2$	1717. $x = 8$	1718. $x = 24$	1719. $x = 7$
1720. $x = 2$	1721. $x = 3$	1722. $x = 5$	1723. $x = 49$

Page 128: Pre-Algebra Equations (One Step) Multiplication and Division

1724. $x = 2$	1725. $x = 7$	1726. $x = 27$	1727. $x = 5$
1728. $x = 4$	1729. $x = 6$	1730. $x = 4$	1731. $x = 3$
1732. $x = 8$	1733. $x = 72$	1734. $x = 2$	1735. $x = 8$
1736. $x = 4$	1737. $x = 9$	1738. $x = 8$	1739. $x = 5$
1740. $x = 7$	1741. $x = 7$	1742. $x = 5$	1743. $x = 8$

Page 129: Pre-Algebra Equations (One Step) Multiplication and Division

1744. $x = 5$	1745. $x = 8$	1746. $x = 4$	1747. $x = 2$
1748. $x = 2$	1749. $x = 24$	1750. $x = 3$	1751. $x = 3$
1752. $x = 7$	1753. $x = 9$	1754. $x = 9$	1755. $x = 30$
1756. $x = 14$	1757. $x = 4$	1758. $x = 3$	1759. $x = 2$
1760. $x = 3$	1761. $x = 8$	1762. $x = 1$	1763. $x = 8$

Page 130: Pre-Algebra Equations (One Step) Multiplication and Division

1764. $x = 4$	1765. $x = 5$	1766. $x = 42$	1767. $x = 2$
1768. $x = 6$	1769. $x = 4$	1770. $x = 1$	1771. $x = 1$
1772. $x = 4$	1773. $x = 2$	1774. $x = 3$	1775. $x = 5$
1776. $x = 6$	1777. $x = 4$	1778. $x = 32$	1779. $x = 7$
1780. $x = 2$	1781. $x = 48$	1782. $x = 5$	1783. $x = 42$

Page 131: Pre-Algebra Equations (One Step) Multiplication and Division

1784. $x = 7$	1785. $x = 4$	1786. $x = 6$	1787. $x = 7$	1788. $x = 5$
1789. $x = 7$	1790. $x = 4$	1791. $x = 8$	1792. $x = 2$	1793. $x = 7$

SUMMER MATH SUCCESS

Name: ________________ Class: __________

1794. $x = 3$ 1795. $x = 8$ 1796. $x = 9$ 1797. $x = 2$ 1798. $x = 8$

1799. $x = 8$ 1800. $x = 4$ 1801. $x = 5$ 1802. $x = 2$ 1803. $x = 3$

Page 132: Pre-Algebra Equations (One Step) Multiplication and Division

1804. $x = 1$ 1805. $x = 6$ 1806. $x = 2$ 1807. $x = 5$

1808. $x = 1$ 1809. $x = 9$ 1810. $x = 5$ 1811. $x = 4$

1812. $x = 9$ 1813. $x = 6$ 1814. $x = 2$ 1815. $x = 81$

1816. $x = 8$ 1817. $x = 4$ 1818. $x = 2$ 1819. $x = 8$

1820. $x = 7$ 1821. $x = 4$ 1822. $x = 8$ 1823. $x = 3$

Page 133: Pre-Algebra Equations (Two Sides)

1824. $x = 8$ 1825. $x = 7$ 1826. $x = 9$ 1827. $x = 9$ 1828. $x = 8$

1829. $x = 4$ 1830. $x = 4$ 1831. $x = 8$ 1832. $x = 3$ 1833. $x = 2$

Page 134: Pre-Algebra Equations (Two Sides)

1834. $x = 9$ 1835. $x = 5$ 1836. $x = 5$ 1837. $x = 9$ 1838. $x = 8$

1839. $x = 6$ 1840. $x = 7$ 1841. $x = 3$ 1842. $x = 2$ 1843. $x = 7$

Page 135: Pre-Algebra Equations (Two Sides)

1844. $x = 8$ 1845. $x = 3$ 1846. $x = 3$ 1847. $x = 4$ 1848. $x = 9$

1849. $x = 4$ 1850. $x = 2$ 1851. $x = 4$ 1852. $x = 5$ 1853. $x = 6$

Page 136: Pre-Algebra Equations (Two Sides)

1854. $x = 3$ 1855. $x = 8$ 1856. $x = 2$ 1857. $x = 5$ 1858. $x = 3$

1859. $x = 6$ 1860. $x = 6$ 1861. $x = 8$ 1862. $x = 5$ 1863. $x = 7$

Page 137: Pre-Algebra Equations (Two Sides)

1864. $x = 3$ 1865. $x = 6$ 1866. $x = 3$ 1867. $x = 5$ 1868. $x = 4$

1869. $x = 9$ 1870. $x = 7$ 1871. $x = 7$ 1872. $x = 7$ 1873. $x = 7$

SUMMER MATH SUCCESS

Name: ____________ Class: ________

Page 138: Pre-Algebra Equations (Two Sides)

1874. $x = 4$ 1875. $x = 9$ 1876. $x = 7$ 1877. $x = 5$ 1878. $x = 4$

1879. $x = 2$ 1880. $x = 7$ 1881. $x = 4$ 1882. $x = 5$ 1883. $x = 9$

Page 139: Pre-Algebra Equations (Two Sides)

1884. $x = 3$ 1885. $x = 8$ 1886. $x = 7$ 1887. $x = 7$ 1888. $x = 5$

1889. $x = 5$ 1890. $x = 2$ 1891. $x = 7$ 1892. $x = 2$ 1893. $x = 3$

Page 140: Pre-Algebra Equations (Two Sides)

1894. $x = 3$ 1895. $x = 5$ 1896. $x = 2$ 1897. $x = 5$ 1898. $x = 7$

1899. $x = 7$ 1900. $x = 9$ 1901. $x = 4$ 1902. $x = 7$ 1903. $x = 9$

Page 141: Pre-Algebra Equations (Two Sides)

1904. $x = 5$ 1905. $x = 4$ 1906. $x = 7$ 1907. $x = 4$ 1908. $x = 8$

1909. $x = 6$ 1910. $x = 9$ 1911. $x = 5$ 1912. $x = 6$ 1913. $x = 4$

Page 142: Pre-Algebra Equations (Two Sides)

1914. $x = 2$ 1915. $x = 2$ 1916. $x = 6$ 1917. $x = 8$ 1918. $x = 2$

1919. $x = 7$ 1920. $x = 7$ 1921. $x = 7$ 1922. $x = 5$ 1923. $x = 9$

Page 143: Simplifying Expressions

1924. $2x + 2$ 1925. $-4x - 15$ 1926. -8

1927. x 1928. $-16x + 19$ 1929. $-10x + 7$

1930. $22x + 16$

Page 144: Simplifying Expressions

1931. $5x - 6$ 1932. $-4x + 9$ 1933. $3x + 9$

1934. $-7x$ 1935. $-12x + 54$ 1936. $20x - 13$

1937. $16x - 1$

Page 145: Simplifying Expressions

1938. $-4x - 9$ 1939. $-14x + 11$ 1940. $4x - 3$

SUMMER MATH SUCCESS

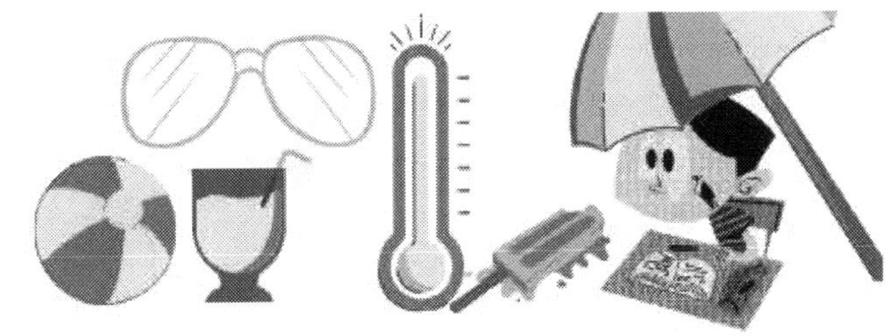

Name: ______________ Class: __________

1941. $15x - 2$
1942. $-18x + 17$
1943. $14x - 12$
1944. $x - 5$

Page 146: Simplifying Expressions

1945. $63x + 41$
1946. $6x + 3$
1947. $-4x - 11$
1948. $6x - 2$
1949. $4x - 10$
1950. $8x - 11$
1951. $35x + 27$

Page 147: Simplifying Expressions

1952. $14x - 4$
1953. $-2x + 5$
1954. $-2x + 8$
1955. $-x + 1$
1956. $x - 3$
1957. $5x - 5$
1958. $23x - 3$

Page 148: Simplifying Expressions

1959. $20x + 10$
1960. $-7x$
1961. $7x$
1962. $5x - 10$
1963. $4x - 6$
1964. $2x + 11$
1965. -2

Page 149: Simplifying Expressions

1966. $-7x$
1967. $4x$
1968. $3x + 4$
1969. $3x + 2$
1970. $14x + 6$
1971. $-4x + 1$
1972. $-12x + 3$

Page 150: Simplifying Expressions

1973. $3x + 1$
1974. $-4x - 11$
1975. $6x + 9$
1976. $3x$
1977. $-7x$
1978. $7x + 3$
1979. $-12x$

Page 151: Simplifying Expressions

1980. $-6x - 5$
1981. $4x - 4$
1982. $-5x - 13$
1983. $-9x + 4$
1984. $7x + 3$
1985. $-7x + 16$
1986. $15x + 1$

SUMMER MATH SUCCESS

Name: ________________ Class: __________

Page 152: Simplifying Expressions

1987. $4x - 2$ 1988. $8x - 16$ 1989. $12x - 3$

1990. $17x + 8$ 1991. x 1992. $-12x + 8$

1993. $7x + 4$

Page 153: Simplifying Expressions

1994. $8x + 4$ 1995. $5x + 12$ 1996. $6x + 7$

1997. $11x + 11$ 1998. $8x - 4$ 1999. $-20x + 17$

2000. $-9x + 2$

Page 154: Simplifying Expressions

2001. $-5x$ 2002. $8x + 3$ 2003. $15x + 14$

2004. $2x - 5$ 2005. $18x - 4$ 2006. $-3x$

2007. $9x + 18$

Page 155: Inequalities - Addition and Subtraction

2008. $x \geq 8$ 2009. $x \leq 7$ 2010. $x > 3$ 2011. $x \geq 9$

2012. $x < 2$ 2013. $x < 16$

Page 156: Inequalities - Addition and Subtraction

2014. $x < 17$ 2015. $x < -3$ 2016. $x \leq -7$ 2017. $x > -6$

2018. $x \geq 6$ 2019. $x > 10$

Page 157: Inequalities - Addition and Subtraction

2020. $x < -4$ 2021. $x \geq 5$ 2022. $x > 1$ 2023. $x > -3$ 2024. $x < -4$

2025. $x < -2$

Page 158: Inequalities - Multiplication and Division

2026. $x < 1/2$ 2027. $x \geq 30$ 2028. $x \leq 32$ 2029. $x \geq 1/3$

2030. $x < 56$ 2031. $x \leq 5/2$

SUMMER MATH SUCCESS

Name: ________ Class: ________

Page 159: Inequalities - Multiplication and Division

2032. $x \leq 3$ **2033.** $x \geq 5/3$ **2034.** $x \leq 21$ **2035.** $x < 4/3$

2036. $x < 49$ **2037.** $x \geq 1/2$

Page 160: Inequalities - Multiplication and Division

2038. $x \geq 12$ **2039.** $x \geq 5/3$ **2040.** $x < 2$ **2041.** $x < 2$

2042. $x \geq 3/4$ **2043.** $x \leq 42$

Page 161: Find the Area and Perimeter

2044. P=33 A=63

2045. P=27 A=35.06

2046. P=58 A=208

2047. P=34 A=48

2048. P=35 A=41.85

2049. P=37 A=60.5

Page 162: Find the Area and Perimeter

2050. P=37 A=81

2051. P=29 A=36

2052. P=43 A=68.04

2053. P=38 A=78

2054. P=48 A=98

2055. P=31 A=40

Page 163: Find the Area and Perimeter

2056. P=35 A=68

2057. P=45 A=97.42

2058. P=19 A=15

2059. P=42 A=87

2060. P=28 A=36.68

2061. P=50 A=104

Page 164: Find the Volume and Surfrace Area

2062. V=65 cm^3 cm^3 SA=79 cm^2 cm^2

2063. V=14 cm^3 cm^3 SA=28 cm^2 cm^2

2064. V=210 cm^3 cm^3 SA=254.0 cm^2 cm^2

2065. V=6 cm^3 cm^3 SA=22.8 cm^2 cm^2

2066. V=6.28 cm^3 cm^3 SA=19 cm^2 cm^2

SUMMER
MATH SUCCESS

Name: ________________ Class: __________

2067. V=112 cm^3 cm^3 SA=144 cm^2 cm^2

Page 165: Find the Volume and Surfrace Area

2068. V=905 cm^3 cm^3 SA=452 cm^2 cm^2

2069. V=113 cm^3 cm^3 SA=113 cm^2 cm^2

2070. V=720 cm^3 cm^3 SA=484 cm^2 cm^2

2071. V=65 cm^3 cm^3 SA=79 cm^2 cm^2

2072. V=230.91 cm^3 cm^3 SA=209 cm^2 cm^2

2073. V=180 cm^3 cm^3 SA=192 cm^2 cm^2

Page 166: Find the Volume and Surfrace Area

2074. V=21 cm^3 cm^3 SA=46 cm^2 cm^2

2075. V=201.06 cm^3 cm^3 SA=201 cm^2 cm^2

2076. V=4 cm^3 cm^3 SA=16.8 cm^2 cm^2

2077. V=549.78 cm^3 cm^3 SA=377 cm^2 cm^2

2078. V=5 cm^3 cm^3 SA=19 cm^2 cm^2

2079. V=20 cm^3 cm^3 SA=50 cm^2 cm^2

Page 167: Calculate the area of each circle.

2080. A=1,017.36 cm^2

2081. A=803.84 cm^2

2082. A=530.66 cm^2

2083. A=907.46 cm^2

2084. A=615.44 cm^2

2085. A=254.34 cm^2

Page 168: Calculate the area of each circle.

2086. A=452.16 cm^2

2087. A=3.14 cm^2

2088. A=113.04 cm^2

2089. A=1,017.36 cm^2

2090. A=78.50 cm^2

2091. A=200.96 cm^2

SUMMER MATH SUCCESS

Name: ________________ Class: __________

Page 169: Calculate the area of each circle.

2092. $A=907.46\ cm^2$
2093. $A=50.24\ cm^2$
2094. $A=12.56\ cm^2$
2095. $A=28.26\ cm^2$
2096. $A=1,017.36\ cm^2$
2097. $A=1,256.00\ cm^2$

Page 170: Calculate the circumference of each circle.

2098. C=119.32 cm
2099. C=6.28 cm
2100. C=37.68 cm
2101. C=75.36 cm
2102. C=31.40 cm
2103. C=69.08 cm

Page 171: Calculate the circumference of each circle.

2104. C=119.32 cm
2105. C=87.92 cm
2106. C=18.84 cm
2107. C=62.80 cm
2108. C=12.56 cm
2109. C=37.68 cm

Page 172: Calculate the circumference of each circle.

2110. C=12.56 cm
2111. C=62.80 cm
2112. C=106.76 cm
2113. C=100.48 cm
2114. C=6.28 cm
2115. C=18.84 cm

Page 173: Measure of Center - Mean

2116. Mean = 57.833
2117. Mean = 66.375
2118. Mean = 46.143
2119. Mean = 39.667
2120. Mean = 61.571
2121. Mean = 54.889

Page 174: Measure of Center - Mean

2122. Mean = 36.571
2123. Mean = 47
2124. Mean = 66.625
2125. Mean = 53.25
2126. Mean = 74.667
2127. Mean = 49.571

Page 175: Measure of Center - Median

2128. Median = 17
2129. Median = 50
2130. Median = 61
2131. Median = 44
2132. Median = 41
2133. Median = 46

SUMMER
MATH SUCCESS

Name: ____________ Class: ________

Page 176: Measure of Center - Median

2134. Median = 44.5
2135. Median = 60.5
2136. Median = 22
2137. Median = 66
2138. Median = 45.5
2139. Median = 20

Page 177: Measure of Center - Mode

2140. Mode = none
2141. Mode = none
2142. Mode = none
2143. Mode = none
2144. Mode = none
2145. Mode = none

Page 178: Measure of Center - Mode

2146. Mode = none
2147. Mode = none
2148. Mode = none
2149. Mode = 18
2150. Mode = 66
2151. Mode = none

Page 179: Measure of Variability - Range

2152. Range = 78
2153. Range = 48
2154. Range = 64
2155. Range = 84
2156. Range = 58
2157. Range = 65

Page 180: Measure of Variability - Range

2158. Range = 60
2159. Range = 68
2160. Range = 73
2161. Range = 77
2162. Range = 78
2163. Range = 86

Made in United States
Orlando, FL
17 June 2024

47975853R00124